Health and social care Intermediate

G
N
V
Q

GUNDEE COLLEGE OF FURTHER EDUCATION

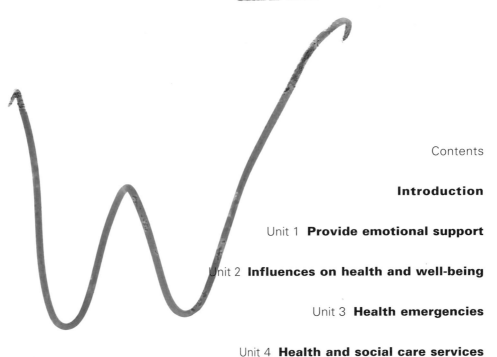

Contents

LONGMAN

This book is part of The Longman Health and Social Care Series

Project Manager   Hugh Hillyard-Parker

Series Editors   Pip Hardy, Hugh Hillyard-Parker, Cathy Lake

Series Consultant   Beryl Stretch   Wirral Metropolitan College
                       Diane Smithson   Hull College

Authors of
these units   Unit 1   *Pip Hardy*
                     Unit 2   *Hugh Hillyard-Parker*
                     Unit 3   *Sheila Simons*
                     Unit 4   *Sheila White*

Advisors and
Critical Readers   Anne Bore   *Beverley College*
                     Alan Gardiner   *Redbridge College*
                     Tanya Hope   *Penwith College, Penzance*
                     Kevin Kendrick   *Liverpool John Moores University*
                     Catherine Lawley   *Redbridge College*
                     Pam Quick   *Hull Colllege*
                     Jane Schober   *De Montfort University*
                     Janet Scott   *Clinical Services Manager, Thanet Healthcare Trust*
                     Julia Wilson   *North Nottinghamshire College*
                     Pam Vincent   *Oxford College*

LONGMAN GROUP LIMITED
Longman House, Burnt Mill, Harlow, Essex, CM20 2JE,
England and Associated Companies throughout the World.

Text © Longman Group 1994

First published 1994
ISBN 0 582 25540 6

Design by Moondisks Ltd, Cambridge.
Set in Univers and New Baskerville in QuarkXpress 3.3 on the Apple Macintosh.
Printed in Great Britain by Butler & Tanner Limited, Frome and London.

The publisher's policy is to use paper manufactured from sustainable forests.

Introduction

This book covers the four mandatory vocational units of the Intermediate GNVQ in Health and Social Care. All the skills, knowledge and understanding outlined in the standards for these, are included in the four chapters. These are briefly described below.

Unit 1: Provide emotional support
Clients of health and care services are particularly vulnerable and need as much support as possible. Good communication is the basis for emotional support.

This unit covers the skills you will need to communicate effectively with clients and colleagues; listening, conversation and questioning skills are used to support both individuals and groups.

Unit 2: Influences on health and well-being
A complex mix of factors affects health and well-being. A recognition of these influences and how they operate in our society is the first step towards being able to make changes which will improve health. This unit considers psychological, social and economic influences and suggests possibilities for promoting good health.

Unit 3: Health emergencies
Everyone is likely to encounter a health emergency at some time in their lives – this unit identifies many of the most common emergency situations and looks at what the non-professional can do to support and help the casualty until first aid arrives. Emphasis is placed on the ability to recognise what is happening and to deal with it appropriately.

Unit 4: Health and social care services
The structure of health and social care in the United Kingdom is vast and complex. Knowledge of what is available and how to gain access to it is invaluable to anyone working in the health and social care field. This unit provides an introduction to the

main providers and looks at how individuals with differing needs can be helped.

Format and approach

This book has been prepared in order to promote active, independent learning. The units are based on the NCVQ Units which form the award and are further subdivided into sections reflecting the elements. Each unit contains, in addition to full coverage of the performance criteria, range and evidence indicators in the standards, a number of activities and projects to encourage you to test out what you know and to think about applications for what you are learning. The activities are self-contained learning tasks which might test new knowledge, involve role-playing, examine previous experience, or encourage group and paired discussion. Projects are larger, research type activities which require you to investigate a particular aspect of the topic you are studying. These are usually linked closely to the evidence indicators for each element.

Core skills

You are encouraged to incorporate core skills into your work on the vocational units. This aim is reflected in the chapters of this book. Projects and activities are constructed in such a way as to ensure adequate opportunity for you to cover core skills. The symbol ⓒ indicates that core skills can be covered by doing the work suggested; the type of core skill covered is indicated by AN (Application of Number), C (Communication) or IT (Information Technology).

Longman Induction booklets

It may be helpful to look at the booklet *Introduction to GNVQ Health and Social Care: Intermediate* before beginning work on the programme. This contains detailed information about GNVQs, their structure, assessment and grading criteria as well as case studies and suggestions of how to approach GNVQ work through the *Longman Study Units.* Students and teachers will find this a helpful introduction to GNVQs in general and to the Health and Social Care programme in particular.

Provide emotional support

GNVQ

Contents

Introduction

'In my experience a good carer is one that makes you feel special – not just one of a bunch of old people in a home. They make you feel they really care about *you*.'

Vi, *resident in a home for elders*

'All carers are busy people, I know, but with some it's as if they're doing you a favour. With others, the really good ones, you feel as if they've all the time in the world for you.'

Shirley, *client with multiple sclerosis*

'For me, the exciting thing about nursing is not just learning how to set up drips and give injections – what makes the job special is the support you can give to people who really need it.'

Eke, *student nurse*

'My son was born with cystic fibrosis. While he was alive – and after he died – I had fantastic support from all sorts of people. I realised what a lifeline that support can be – which is why I decided to train as a care worker myself.'

Carl, *studying for a GNVQ in Health and Care*

As these short quotations show, there is a lot more to being a carer than being skilled in practical tasks. The practical skills are important, of course, but really successful carers are those that combine them with a positive, caring attitude.

This unit focuses on the emotional side of caring – the more intangible skills you need in order to support individuals. Much of this unit, therefore, is about good communication. You will look at communication from both sides: how to listen as well as how to talk.

The unit is divided into three main sections, each focusing on one aspect of giving emotional support:

- using **conversational techniques** to maintain social interaction
- helping to meet people's needs for **self-esteem**
- showing **supportive behaviour** both in individual and group situations.

Communicating effectively with others

Communication is a two-way process – it is about giving and receiving information, thoughts, ideas and feelings. This means it involves both *sending* and *receiving* messages.

The first section of this study unit looks at some of the techniques you need to communicate effectively with other people. You will investigate techniques of active listening. You will also think about the hidden messages people send through body language.

The value of listening

If communication is a two-way process, then effective listening is clearly just as important as talking.

Activity

Either individually, or as a group, think about four or five occasions in the last day or two when it was important for you to listen. Make a list of who you were listening to and say why it was important to listen. For example:

Who I was listening to

Why I should listen

Lesson with teacher about health emergencies

To learn how to recognise situations that are emergencies

As you probably found, listening is important in all sorts of situations:

- at school or college when talking to teachers and other students
- in your own family
- when you go to the shops or the post office
- when talking to friends.

You may need to listen for a number of reasons:

- to gain information
- to receive instructions
- to get to know other people
- to give encouragement or support to other people
- to show your interest in others
- just for fun – because you are enjoying a conversation.

Now think about why listening is important in care work. Imagine yourself working as a care worker who visits clients in their own homes. Work through the list of reasons for listening given above and give examples of when someone in this job would need to listen. For example:

Reason for listening	When to listen
To gain information	from my manager, for example about which clients to visit, what help they might need
	from clients, for example about how well they are feeling, what help they actually need

Listening is a particularly important skill for care workers, because clients often need particular *support* from care staff. This is partly because they are more **dependent** on others for help, because of illness, frailty or disability. They may be feeling vulnerable, or even depressed.

If clients feel they are being listened to by care staff, they are more likely to feel valued and cared for. Similarly, if people feel they are *not* being listened to, they may get a message telling them that they are *not worth* listening to.

Barriers to listening

Listening is not always simple. It takes time and effort – and interest. It is all too easy to pretend to listen rather than to listen actively.

You will have had conversations with people where you felt the other person wasn't listening. You may have felt they:

- were too busy to be bothered with what you had to say

- were concentrating on something else

- had strong feelings about what you were saying, so didn't want to hear your point of view

- just wanted you to finish speaking so that they could tell you something they were bursting to say.

Now answer the following questions.

1 **How could you tell from their behaviour that they were not listening?**

2 **What could they have done instead to show they were listening?**

There are all sorts of ways that people show they are not listening. They do this by:

- interrupting you

- looking in the other direction or avoiding eye contact

- carrying on doing something else while talking to you

- changing the subject

- talking about themselves all the time

- contradicting you aggressively.

It is easy to blame other people when a conversation seems unsatisfactory. However, we all have our own particular listening weaknesses. If we can identify them then we can start to deal with them.

Active listening

Being a good listener takes skill and practice. You not only have to *hear* the words people are saying, you have to *understand* them. This means making a conscious effort to avoid the barriers listed above. When you achieve this, then listening becomes an *active* process.

Active listening means:

- allowing the other person to finish what they want to say

- focusing on the person speaking, for example making eye contact

- stopping what you are doing to listen to the person

- encouraging the other person to continue, for example by nodding or making encouraging noises like 'uh huh'

- keeping to the subject and not diverting to other topics

- not bringing in personal feelings and personal experiences unless they become relevant to the conversation.

In the normal rules of conversation we take turns at speaking and listening. We also alternate topics so that there is a balance – between what you want to talk about and what the other person wants to say.

In care work active listening often means tipping the balance in favour of the client: you focus on the client and give priority to what *the client* is saying.

Showing interest

Active listening draws you into the other person's world. When this happens you actually become more interested in what the other person is saying.

Activity

Read through the following dialogue which describes an everyday conversation between a client, Harry, an 87-year-old retired postal worker, and Donna, a domiciliary care assistant who visits him at home.

Donna: 'Hello, Harry!'

Harry: 'Hello, Donna. Isn't it a beautiful day today? Is it nice out?'

Donna: *(hanging her coat up)* 'Yes, it's lovely. Do you enjoy being outdoors?'

Harry: 'Oh yes, I used to go hill-walking when I was younger.'

Donna: *(turns and looks at Harry)* 'You used to go hill-walking? That sounds energetic!'

Harry: 'Not half. We'd sometimes walk twenty miles a day – me and Helen – my wife.'

Donna: 'Twenty miles! You must have been really fit.'

Harry: 'Oh yes. It was great. I couldn't manage that now, of course, but we used to see some wonderful places – the Yorkshire Dales, Dartmoor, the Highlands. You name it, we walked it!'

How did Donna show that she was listening actively? Identify at least three things she did. What is the effect of the conversation – what do you think Harry and Donna gained from it? Do you think they enjoyed it?

Donna certainly used her skills to encourage and respond positively to Harry as he talked about his past interest in hill-walking. She stopped to give her full attention to him. She picked up on the topic of hill-walking and she followed up with questions that encouraged him to talk more. Harry enjoyed talking about happy times he had in the past and Donna should also have enjoyed building up a picture of Harry as a younger man.

There are three skills which are particularly helpful in showing interest and understanding: **reflection, interpretation** and **paraphrasing.** Donna used some of these skills and we will consider them in more detail now.

Reflection

Reflective listening means repeating back to the person what they have said – as though you were a mirror. Donna used this technique when she reflected Harry's words by saying: 'You used to go hill-walking?'.

The technique of reflecting is useful in many different situations:
- It encourages the other person to talk further.
- It helps you check that you have understood correctly what someone else is saying.

- It shows to the person who is speaking that you have understood, are interested and are listening.
- It keeps conversation going if you don't know quite how to respond.

Reflecting is a useful technique when someone says something you may find challenging or even shocking, and you don't know what the best response is.

> **Activity**
>
> Imagine you are caring for a woman who is being treated for rheumatoid arthritis. One day she says to you:
> 'It gets so painful that I don't know what to do with myself. I feel like just ending it all.'
>
> Could you use the technique of reflection in this situation? Why would it be useful? What would you say?

Reflection could well be useful in this situation. You have been presented with a challenging statement and may not be sure how to react. Is your client really serious or is she joking? Or is it a way of asking for help? You may not be able to tell. If you reflect back her last words in a concerned or questioning tone of voice – 'you feel like ending it all?' – you are asking your client to tell you more.

Paraphrasing

Paraphrasing is similar to reflecting but you use your own words to summarise what your client has said.

> **Activity**
>
> Which of the following responses do you think is a good example of paraphrasing?
>
> *Client*:
> 'It's really hot in here. It always feels so hot and stuffy – it makes me feel really ill. I just can't breathe.'
>
> *Carer*:
> 1 'Why don't you go outside – it's quite cool out on the porch.'
> 2 'You find the atmosphere in here oppressive?'
> 3 'Would you like me to open a window?'

Paraphrasing is used in the second response: the carer summarises the client's feelings and shows that he/she has understood what the client is saying. The first response is inappropriate and off-hand. The third response is an example of interpretation.

Interpretation

Interpretation goes one stage further by looking for the *hidden meaning* of what people say. You reply by saying what you think they meant rather than what they actually said. In the activity above, the client complains of feeling hot and stuffy; he/she may be *implying* that he/she wants a window opened, or even that he/she wants to spend more time in the garden.

Activity

Which of Carol's responses to Jake's statement is an example of interpretation?

Jake: 'I really hate it when my girlfriend spends time with Peter. But then I think that's stupid – they're in the same band and she has a right to talk to him. But I feel so angry when I see them together – and then I feel unreasonable.'

Carol: 1 'Everybody feels like that sometimes.'

2 'You feel jealous when your girlfriend is with Peter, but you don't like feeling that way.'

3 'You feel jealous when your girlfriend spends time with other people.'

The second response is the one which most closely *interprets* Jake's feelings. The first response is less than helpful, while the third response doesn't appreciate that Jake does not like his feelings of jealousy.

These responsive listening techniques are very useful in any situation, but can be especially useful in conversations with clients. They are powerful ways of showing clients, who may be feeling vulnerable or anxious, that you are listening to them and understand what they are telling you.

There are no hard and fast guidelines about when you should use these different techniques. Sometimes it will be appropriate just to reflect someone's words and encourage him/her to talk on; at other times paraphrasing or interpreting will help you move the conversation forward more positively.

2.1, 2.2 C **C** **Project**

For this project you will need two other people, preferably students studying for this GNVQ unit. Two of you are to talk for up to two minutes about a topic you agree in advance, for example why you are interested in caring for people and are studying for this GNVQ. Each of you should use the skills of reflecting, paraphrasing and interpreting to show that you are listening to, and understanding, what the other person is saying.

The third person will be an *observer* who watches you both talking and then gives you *feedback* about how you used each technique. Before you start, agree on a checklist of the techniques and points you want to cover. The observer can tick off the points as each of the talkers demonstrate the techniques.

When each of you has had a turn listening, speaking and observing, discuss how the conversations went. As a speaker, did you feel that your listener heard you accurately and responded appropriately? What made you feel this? Note down your thoughts and impressions and how you felt.

If you have access to the equipment you could tape record or video yourselves. This tape, plus your completed checklists and notes, will provide evidence of your conversational skills.

Non-verbal communication

Much of our communication takes place without words. Good communication means being aware of unspoken messages; that is, tuning in to what is *not* said as well as what *is* said.

The next activity will help you to discover how important it is to use our bodies to emphasise the words we choose.

Activity

For this activity you will need the help of a friend or another student. You are to have a discussion about what you did the evening before. You are to use techniques of active listening, while your friend must adhere to the following rules:

- keep his/her arms folded
- don't look at the other person
- frown throughout the whole conversation.

Now talk for up to a minute. At the end of the 'conversation' both of you should say how successful you felt the conversation was.

You probably both found the conversation highly unsatisfactory. You were receiving constant negative feedback as you spoke. You may have received the message that you were not worth listening to or even that you were 'invisible'.

It was your friend's **body language** that made you feel this. Many people in care feel that they are treated like 'invisible' people and that their opinions and feelings are ignored.

What is non-verbal communication?

Non-verbal communication (or body language) is any way of communicating that does not use words. The last activity showed how powerful this form of communication can be.

Activity

The next time you have a conversation with someone, watch their hands. Most people find it quite difficult to talk without using gestures to reinforce what they are saying.

Non-verbal communication sends us clear messages, if we know how to interpret them. These messages may either reinforce or contradict spoken communication.

Activity

Here are some typical non-verbal messages. Look at
each picture and describe the message you think is
being conveyed. If possible, discuss your answers with
other students.

In Britain, most people would interpret the body language in the following ways:

1 two people standing close to each other may suggest intimidation; on the other hand it may suggest affection
2 the person is relaxed
3 this posture shows attentiveness or interest
4 surprise, alarm or terror
5 sadness, depression
6 happiness or joy
7 anger
8 what does this blank face show – boredom, thoughtfulness, who knows?
9 looking away or at the floor may show embarrassment
10 this is an open gesture perhaps offering something
11 waving indicates welcome or pleasure at seeing someone, or may mean 'goodbye'
12 bowing is usually a mark of respect
13 kissing a cheek suggests affection or respect
14 touching an arm indicates concern or care
15 putting an arm round someone usually means friendship, support.

If you compare your answers with those of a friend, you may find that you interpreted the body language in different ways. Some differences in interpretation depend on the **culture** we come from.

Contradictory messages

Look back at the first picture in the last activity. While holding a normal conversation most British people keep about a metre of space between themselves and the other person. In other countries people feel comfortable with less space. The same may apply to touch. For example, the gesture shown in picture 14 may show concern in Britain; in other countries, such as Italy, it often shows just friendship.

Other examples of cultural differences in body language are described below:

- In some Indian societies, women do not make eye contact with men, even with those they know well or to whom they are related.

- In Britain a sharp intake of breath suggests surprise, amazement or even horror; in Sweden it indicates agreement or approval.

- In some Asian countries, moving the head from side to side means 'yes'. However, this movement is very similar to the shake of the head which means 'no' in other cultures.

These **contradictory messages** can be confusing in any situation, not least in the care setting. If you are talking to or caring for someone from a different cultural group, you cannot make assumptions about their behaviour which are based on your own culture.

Non-verbal communication can be particularly important when caring for others. Many people in care have difficulties with spoken communication which makes it hard for others to understand them. This may be because:

- they may have speech or hearing difficulties
- they may have an illness or disability which makes it hard or tiring to speak
- English is not their first language.

In all these cases clients may use non-verbal communication to express their needs. In return you may also use non-verbal forms of communication to show that you have understood or to ask for more information.

Project

Carry out some research into non-verbal communication.

1 Sit somewhere in a public place and watch people talking and relating to each other. Make a note of any body language they use. How do they use body language to communicate messages to other people? Present your observations as a short report, focusing on the different forms of body language discussed earlier.

2 Arrange to video a TV programme – preferably an interview or documentary. Watch it once through and be aware of how people use body language. Then watch the programme a second time with the sound turned off, so that you can concentrate on the body language. Make a note of what you felt the body language meant and how you responded to it. Your commentary may be tape recorded or written down as notes.

Think about how you will carry out this project and record your ideas in an action plan.

Encouraging conversation

You have seen how you can encourage conversation by using active listening and non-verbal communication. Another effective strategy is to use questions.

Asking questions can encourage the people you are talking with to explain their meaning; they can help you to check that you understand them. Some people need a lot of encouragement in the form of questions to enable them to talk.

'Open' and 'closed' questions

Like other aspects of communication, using questions requires skill and practice. How you phrase a question can determine what response you get. Some questions encourage people to open up and talk: these are called 'open' questions; other questions discourage people from talking further: these are called 'closed' questions. In short:

- An 'open' question is any question that cannot be answered by saying simply 'yes' or 'no', or an equally short answer – the person has to expand further.
- A 'closed' question is one that demands only a 'yes' or 'no' or similar short answer.

Compare the following responses to two similar questions:

Open:

Q How are you feeling today?

A Well, not too bad really. My back is a bit painful, but the arthritis in my knee is much better.

Closed:

Q Are you feeling better today?

A No.

Activity

Read through the following list of questions and decide which are open and which are closed.

1 How does that feel?

2 Does that hurt?

3 Where does it hurt?

4 I wonder which dress you would like to wear?

5   Would you like to wear this dress today?

6   What would you like to do today?

7   Would you like to go for a walk today?

8   What did you think of the film last night?

9   Did you like the film last night?

Are open questions always better than closed questions? Can you think of a situation where a closed question is actually the most appropriate type to ask?

In a lot of social situations, open questions are the most appropriate as they help the conversation develop. However, closed questions can be very useful for gaining specific information, such as where or when something happened. If you are not careful, though, they can shut down the conversation altogether.

In the last activity you probably identified that questions **1**, **3**, **4**, **6** and **8** are open ones and **2**, **5**, **7** and **9** are closed ones.

Sequences, probes and prompts

A series of thoughtful, open questions will encourage people to think things through and follow a train of thought. Asking a series or a sequence of questions can help draw out people, especially if they are feeling shy, or confused, or vulnerable. Read through the following example of a conversation between Paul, a care worker, and Mr Havel, one of his clients.

Paul: 'Good morning, Mr Havel. How are you today?'

Mr Havel: 'All right, I suppose.'

Paul: 'How did you sleep last night?'

Mr Havel: 'Not very well.'

Paul: 'Oh, I'm sorry. Why couldn't you sleep?'

Mr Havel: 'I don't know... Well... I suppose I'm a bit worried about how I'm going to manage.'

Paul: '...how you're going to manage?'

Mr Havel: 'Yes, things just go round and round in my head.'

Paul: 'Is there something particular bothering you?'

Mr Havel: 'Well, yes, it's money really. With interest rates falling, I'm getting much less interest on my savings. I don't know how I'll cope.'

In a series of only a few questions, Paul has encouraged Mr Havel to talk about a problem that is causing him real anxiety. Simply talking about the problem may make Mr Havel feel better; if Mr Havel has real financial difficulties, Paul may be able to alert other people who can help or advise him.

As this example shows, you can ask questions that move from the more general, for example 'how are you today', to the more specific, for example 'is there something that is bothering you?'. This technique is sometimes called **funnelling.**

Activity

What other techniques did Paul use to keep the conversation going and promote interaction with Mr Havel?

Paul has used gentle probing to get exact information about what is bothering Mr Havel. He also used reflection ('…how you're going to manage?') at a point when he wasn't sure how to respond.

Silence

There is one other conversational technique that needs to be mentioned: that is being silent. Many people see silences as 'holes' in conversation that have to be filled. On the contrary, silences may help conversations develop in many ways. People use silence to:

- gather their thoughts before saying anything else
- assess how you have reacted to what they have said so far
- wait for some sign of encouragement from you – either verbal or non-verbal
- work out the best way of expressing what they are going to say next.

Don't be afraid of silence – it is often a helpful space which others can choose to fill or to leave empty.

Respecting individuals

Throughout this unit so far we have stressed the need, in health and care work, to treat people as individuals. But what does this mean? What things help people to feel individual?

Activity

**What factors make you feel you are an individual?
If possible, answer this question together with a group of
other people, for example students on your study
programme. Make a list of the main points.**

It is impossible to pin down exactly what makes us feel individual, but
there are factors that many people think are important:
• feeling there are things that are different or unique about us
• having a sense of our own worth or value
• being important or special to other people
• a feeling of belonging – to a family, group, culture.

A range of other factors may make up our individuality.
These include gender, age, interests, religion, cultural background,
physical and mental abilities.

**Caring for
individuals**

We often talk about people who need care as being 'clients'.
We then talk about them collectively as 'client groups', 'the elderly',
'people with disabilities' or 'the mentally ill'. It can be dangerous
to lump people together in this way, so that clients are seen not as
individuals, but as a group of people who all have the same needs.

Activity

**Look at the following three illustrations of care situations
where care workers make inappropriate attempts at
communication. What do they do wrong? How are they
denying the clients' individuality?**

**Now look back at the short conversations described
earlier between Donna and Harry, and Paul and Mr Havel.
Do you think the carers, Donna and Paul, treated their
clients as individuals? If so, how did they do it?**

18

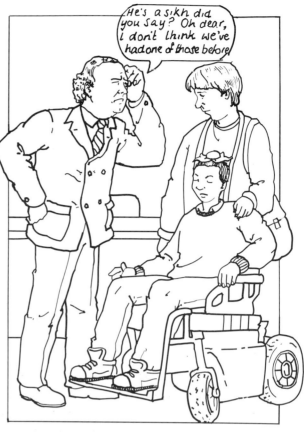

In all three situations illustrated on page 19 the client's individuality is being denied:

1 Mrs Eastman is not a medical procedure; she is a woman with a host of individual needs and preferences.

2 The Sikh boy in the wheelchair is having at least two aspects of his individuality ignored. By talking above his head, the care worker is assuming he is not capable of communicating effectively with him. He also views his Sikhism as something new and difficult, not as a part of his individuality.

3 Here the care home manager makes the decision in a bossy fashion that two elderly people should not be allowed to have the same room and enjoy a loving, sexual relationship. She is making assumptions about them and denying their emotional needs.

Unfortunately situations like these are all too common.

On the other hand, Donna and Paul did treat their clients as individuals. They did this by communicating effectively with them, and by showing interest, concern and respect for the person they were talking to. The next section of this unit looks in more detail at this aspect of providing emotional support.

2.1, 2.2 C Ⓒ **Project**

This project needs to be organised with your study group as a whole. Arrange to carry out role-plays of an interview. Select one person to be the interviewee and two or three others to be the interviewing panel. Decide on what the interview situation will be. It could be:

- a mock job interview, say for a position as a care worker or any other job
- an interview to get onto the GNVQ study programme
- a mock TV interview on a topical issue.

Carry out an interview for a period of, say, 10 minutes. Each interviewer is to pay particular attention to:

- using questioning techniques
- respecting the individuality of the interviewee
- using body language.

Carry out this role-play in the presence of your teacher or trainer who may be able to use the session as part of your assessment. You may also choose to write up a short report or review of the session.

Building people's self-esteem

In the first section of this unit you looked in detail at communication skills. You will now go on to investigate how you can apply these skills in a constructive way to help build people's self-esteem. This is an important aspect of care work, as well as an essential part of building any relationship.

What is self-esteem?

Self-esteem refers to your sense of your own worth and value. It is closely related to the view you have of yourself and what you see as being your identity or **self image**. Self-esteem is determined to some extent by how other people react to you.

All sorts of other things can influence your sense of worth, including present circumstances, past experiences and things you know are coming up in the future.

Activity

Take a moment to think about your own self-esteem. What are the things that give you a sense of your own value? You may think, for example, about how well you get on with people, how good you are at a sport you enjoy, how good you are at school or college work. Make some notes under the heading: 'What builds my self-esteem'.

If possible, compare your ideas with those of a friend or someone you trust. Can you agree on factors that are important to both of you? Are there some which one of you considers important, but the other does not?

There are all sorts of things that can contribute to your sense of self-esteem:

• skills – the things you are good at, for example playing an instrument, cooking, your studies

• appearance – feeling smart, fashionable, attractive

• achievements – the successes you have had in your life

• job – satisfaction gained from a fulfilling working life

• life-style – choices you make about how you live and what you do in your life

• culture or background – influences in your family and community that have helped form your individuality and that you are proud of

• religion – having the security or joy of religious faith.

You probably discovered some similarities and some differences in your views of yourselves; these may have to do with your particular background and approach to life. Provided that they are aware of our strengths and can build on them, most people can accept their weaknesses without too much loss of self-esteem.

If there are changes in your abilities or in other people's reactions to you, your self-esteem is likely to suffer.

Activity

Imagine yourself in the following situations. How do you think these changes in circumstance would affect your self-esteem?

1 **Sport is a very important part of your life, but you break your leg so that you are unable to play for six weeks.**

2 **A long-standing and very close friend seems to 'drop' you for some new friends.**

In both these situations your self-esteem may well be lowered for the following reasons:

1 You may feel useless and left out if you can't join in with the sport you are so passionate about.

2 You may feel hurt and wonder why your 'friend' now prefers other people's company.

While your self-esteem is lowered, your *need* for self-esteem remains the same, but this need is not being met. These feelings can easily lead to frustration or cause you to behave in a way which suggests lack of confidence. This may then lead other people to lower their opinion of your abilities.

However, people who know and value you are likely to be aware of changes in your self-esteem. If they care for you they will try to help you find new or different ways of meeting your self-esteem needs.

Clients' self-esteem needs

Helping people meet their self-esteem needs is an important part of any health or care professional's job. Self-esteem is important for all of us, but can be a particular issue for people who need care.

Activity

Read through the following two descriptions of people receiving care and consider the following questions.

- How might their self-esteem be affected by their situations?
- What self-esteem needs do you think they may have?

1 **Enid is an elderly widow who has lived alone since her husband died. Three months ago she had a stroke which severely affected her right side. Living alone was no longer possible, so she moved**

to a home called 'The Poplars'. She used to work as a solicitor's clerk, a job she loved, and has two children and four grandchildren, all of whom live a long way away.

2 Geoff is a young man with AIDS. He comes into hospital from time to time to recover from illnesses he contracts, where you help care for him. His partner died recently of an AIDS-related illness. He was dismissed from his last job when they heard about his partner's death.

Both these individuals have had to deal with major events threatening their self-esteem:

- illness and the threat of death
- loss of a loved one and the feelings of love and security they had shared
- loss of independence
- loss of a job.

The need for care can itself affect people's self-esteem. It may be associated with other factors that prevent self-esteem needs being met. In Geoff's case, for example, the stigma attached to having AIDS has led to other blows, such as the loss of his job. These blows have caused other self-esteem needs to be taken away.

Some people who have received care all their lives have never had any self-esteem, particularly if they have lived in institutions. They may have become **institutionalised**. This means they have learned to rely totally on the routines of the institution to meet their needs; they may find it impossible to express any of their own individual needs.

Identifying self-esteem needs

In the last activity you probably found it hard to tell what Enid's and Geoff's self-esteem needs are – you do not have a lot of information about them and you cannot see them or talk to them. In order to find out what self-esteem needs individuals have, you have to employ a range of skills. These include:

- skills of observation
- conversational skills.

Using observational skills

Making observations is an important part of care work. Some observations you make are straightforward, for example has a wound stopped bleeding or healed up? Care workers also have to make less clear-cut observations, focusing on people's behaviour, needs or emotions. Identifying people's self-esteem needs falls into this grey area.

Activity

Either individually or in a group, discuss the following questions:

- In what ways can people's *appearances* give you information about them and what self-esteem needs they may have?
- Think about yourself. How could someone meeting you for the first time get a good idea, from your *appearance*, of what factors contribute to your self-esteem?
- In what ways can people's *behaviour* give you information about them and what self-esteem needs they may have?

Our appearance does give out a lot of information. Most of us make conscious choices about the sorts of clothes we wear, for example, or how we cut our hair, or what make-up, if any, we wear. We deliberately send out messages saying, for example, 'I care about fashion', 'I identify with a particular group', or even 'I don't care about appearances'. These messages give other people clues about what we think is important in our lives.

Behaviour also gives clear messages about us. You have already looked at ways in which body language gives information. That is only one aspect of behaviour. Everything we do gives clues to other people, for example whether we behave calmly or quietly, whether we make a lot of noise and shout. Being aware of the messages people give, through keen and sensitive observation, will help you interpret the clues.

Avoiding stereotypes

It is important to recognise that there are dangers in making judgements purely on observation. It is very common in our society to try to fit people into categories – to give them labels. For example someone may be labelled as 'a single mother' or 'gay' or 'black'. The danger is that once a label is applied, people think that the label completely describes that person.

Activity

The following are words that are used to describe people. How you could tell, on a first meeting, if someone was:

• gay • a single mother • depressed • deaf • a Muslim • a Roman Catholic?

If you *could* tell that someone was any of the things listed, what would that tell you about that person?

You might be tempted to say that you could tell just by looking.

- Two men or two women with their arms linked together may well be gay – then again, they may be just good friends.
- Someone who is depressed may look unhappy and tired – but equally, many depressed people put on a brave face to the world while visiting their doctors with symptoms of clinical depression.
- Many Muslim women wear scarves and other distinctive clothes, but many do not. Many Muslims, like many Christians and Jews, do not observe religious rites and customs.

Observation may give you information, but it may be information that is *inaccurate, incomplete* or *misleading*. For example, if you do find out that someone is gay, what does that tell you about that person's self-esteem needs in areas such as religion, money, cultural identity, academic or other achievements? It does not tell you anything.

In short, you cannot make assumptions about people simply on the basis of what they *appear* to be. To gain a true picture of people, you need to talk to them as individuals – asking them questions and listening to the answers. Using conversational techniques will help you achieve this.

Recognising individuals

As you have seen, caring for people involves recognising them as individuals, not just as people needing care. Give a little more thought to what makes people unique and different.

Activity

Write down the names and details of five people you know whose backgrounds or lifestyles may be different from yours. List the things you have in common and briefly note what makes that person different from you. For example,

Title	Name	Age	Place of birth	Religion	Occupation	Medical needs
Miss	Lucksan Avisit	27	Bangkok	Buddhist	left school at 10	Diabetes

We are both women and she wanted to be a nurse as well. She was the oldest in her family like I am. She was born in Thailand and is a practising Buddhist – those are differences. But I'm a Christian so religion is important to both of us.

Doing this activity should have made you more aware of the similarities and differences between people and the importance of seeing people as individuals. As their carer, it is important to get to know them, talk and listen to them, gather information about them and then respond in a way which makes them feel valued as individuals.

Helping others to achieve high self-esteem

Building up people's self-esteem is an important part of care work, just as it is in all relationships. As with other aspects of communication, there are specific skills and techniques you can use to do this.

The following guidelines suggest the most important points to remember when helping others improve their self-esteem.

- *Let people know they are valued* – this will help them to value themselves.
- *Listen and talk to people* – offering your time, show respect for and interest in their opinions and experiences.
- *Recognise people's efforts and achievements* – most people respond to praise and encouragement and want to build on their success.
- *Ask and talk about people's past experiences* – show clients that you see them as real people and can accept and cope with the painful parts of their lives as well as the more cheerful parts.
- *Enjoy what is different about people* – in your role as a carer you can enjoy finding out about other people, their culture, beliefs, identity, and so on.
- *Allow people to make choices and decisions* – this helps to give clients control over their own lives and shows your faith in their ability to do this.

Activity

Look back at the case studies of Enid and Geoff on pages 23–24. How could you use the techniques listed on the previous page to help meet their self-esteem needs?

As a carer for Enid or Geoff you can play a significant part in helping meet some of their self-esteem needs. There are some needs you cannot meet, like Enid's need for independence or Geoff's need for a job, but there are areas where carers can make a significant impact. These are areas connected with their sense of individuality, identity, value and support. For example:

- Enid may feel lonely, even bewildered. She has lost her husband, her home, and her ability to look after herself. You can show her that you value her as an individual. You can show interest in her, her past accomplishments and her family. You can help her practically by helping her to relearn skills she has lost due to her stroke. You can also listen to her patiently as she talks about how frustrating she finds her disability.

- Geoff, as well as being bereaved, has suffered discrimination for being gay and may not feel able to grieve openly. He needs to be helped to mourn his partner – you can help him by encouraging him to talk openly and by recognising his feelings of loss. Geoff may also need to express his anger about the loss of his job.

To achieve these goals, you need to be skilled – as well as patient and sensitive. These are some of the hallmarks of good carers.

Activity

Read through the following list of skills. They all refer to ways of encouraging successful conversations. They are certainly useful in working with clients and they are also useful in any area of your life. Try to think of one recent example of how you have used each skill. If you cannot think of an example this may be a point you need to focus on in future conversations.

Structuring a conversation

Starting a conversation	finding an appropriate remark or approach to get into conversation
Developing the conversation	going beyond initial polite comments or small-talk; using the conversational techniques listed below
Finishing the conversation	finding an appropriate way to round off the conversation, for example saying how you've enjoyed talking to the person and that you look forward to speaking again later

Using conversational techniques

Listening	applying the skills of active listening (see page 5)
Interpreting body language	understanding the non-verbal messages, for example sensing if people may be unhappy although they say they're fine
Questioning	using questions, probes and prompts to encourage conversation

Other conversational approaches

Asking for help	for example, getting someone to teach you a skill he/she has which you don't have
Expressing a compliment	for example, saying that you think someone is good at telling a story
Expressing affection	for example, saying or showing that you care for someone and enjoy his/her company
Responding to anger	for example, allowing someone to express his/her feelings and not trying to change the subject

You may not feel that you are always in command of all these skills. However, with practice almost everyone can become good at these things. Learning how to do so will not only help you meet your clients' needs but will also improve your own sense of achievement – and self-esteem!

Project

This project will give you an opportunity to practise the conversational skills which you worked on earlier in this section in order to meet clients' self-esteem needs.
You will need to work in pairs to carry out a role-play.

There are two scenarios:

1 A One person plays the role of a new student joining a study group half-way through the term; nobody knows anything about this new student.

B The other person plays the role of one of the other students in the group.

2 A One person plays the role of a new patient who has just been admitted on to a busy general surgery ward of a hospital.

B The other person plays a nursing assistant on the ward.

The aim of this role-play is for one person (in each case B) to start a conversation with the 'new student' or 'new patient' (A) and use conversational skills to identify some of the newcomer's self-esteem needs.

The person playing the part of the student or patient should make a list beforehand of the things that are most important to his/her self-esteem. The list should also include notes about how he/she is feeling at the moment, for example anxious, nervous, keen to make new friends.

Each person in the pair should have a chance to be either the new student or the new patient. The conversation should last about five minutes and, for this exercise, it is up to the B person to take the lead in starting, developing and finishing the conversation. This person should use as many of the conversational techniques and approaches as he/she thinks appropriate for the situation.

At the end of the role-plays, assess how successful the conversation was. Did person A feel that his/her self-esteem needs were identified? Did person A feel better or reassured at the end of the conversation? Use the checklist on page 29 to assess how well person B used the conversational techniques and approaches listed there.

3

Supporting individuals and groups

In the previous two sections you have looked at conversation techniques and how you can use them to promote self-esteem in other people. In this section we will go on to look at how your communication skills can be used to *support* people.

Situations where you need support

Support is something that everyone needs. No matter how strong individuals may feel, no matter how independent they appear, they need support.

Activity

- What support do you need in your work? Make a list of the support you need in order to complete your GNVQ.
- Can you think of times in your studies when you might need (or have needed) more support than others?
- Who do you turn to for support? Do you think you get all the support you need?

To complete your GNVQ you probably need lots of support, from:
- family – to give you time and space to do all the work you have to do
- teachers and tutors – to give you guidance on how to approach activities and projects
- fellow students – to share ideas and tasks
- friends – to talk over problems and to have a shoulder to cry on!

You need more support at some times than at others. Perhaps your work isn't going well – you can't get to grips with it, or you feel overwhelmed. You may be having family or relationship problems which are affecting your work.

In these situations you may turn to other people to talk over difficulties, review the situation and look for ways of solving problems.

Giving support is a part of all sorts of relationships:

• friendship • family relationships • the teacher – student relationship.

In some relationships we expect to give support as well as to receive it. For example, we know that our friends will listen to us and help us. In return we are there to do the same for them.

Giving support is also an integral part of the relationship between carer and client. It is one of the most important and rewarding aspects of the jobs of all care professionals.

Support in the care setting

Start this section by reading the following case study.

> Ruth was very nervous as she lay in her hospital bed. She was going over in her mind what she wanted to ask the doctor about her operation the following day. When he came to her bedside he had four young students with him. He did explain about the operation and he even asked her if she had any questions, but Ruth just clammed up. Then he was gone, and Ruth felt frustrated and foolish.

Ruth needed support in this situation – and its outcome suggests that she didn't get it. What happened?

Activity

1 **Think about why Ruth felt so vulnerable. List all the reasons you can think of.**

2 **Consider why the care staff were not as helpful as they could have been.**

You may have thought that Ruth felt vulnerable because:

• she was in a strange environment and lying down in bed wearing only a nightdress
• a lot of people were looking down at her
• she felt nervous of the doctor because he is a professional and she didn't want to waste his time.

The doctor may not have been able to help because:

• he was very busy – he may have been overworked
• he may have been running late

- he was trying to teach at the same time as talking to Ruth
- he may never have been in hospital as a patient himself.

The students may not have been able to help because:
- they didn't feel able to act without the doctor's permission
- they felt nervous
- they didn't want to waste the doctor's time.

As you have already seen, people who need or receive care often feel vulnerable or threatened and need extra support. Ruth certainly falls into this category.

Caring for others involves making contact with people – showing them warmth and concern, and helping them practically and emotionally. In this case the doctor certainly did his duty but, for whatever reason, he did not offer the support Ruth needed.

What is supportive behaviour?

You have thought about when you need and give support, but how do you show supportive behaviour?

Activity

Which of the following examples of behaviour do you think could be called supportive? Can you think of a situation when the behaviour described would be supportive?

1 agreeing with everything someone says

2 pointing out flaws or things which have been overlooked

3 simply being there

4 encouraging people to talk when they want to

5 allowing people to be silent when they want to

6 asking lots of questions and attempting to find out more

7 listening attentively

8 waiting for people to talk when they are ready

9 steering away from painful or difficult subjects

10 continually bringing up painful or difficult subjects

11 being honest

12 saying what you think the other person wants you to say.

There are many forms of **supportive behaviour** but usually such behaviour shows sincerity, warmth and understanding. The behaviour in points **3**, **4**, **5**, **6**, **7**, **8**, and **11** could all be described as supportive.

Point **9** could also be supportive as long as you don't appear simply not to be interested.

People need different kinds of support at different times. The support they need may be:

- practical
- social
- emotional.

For example, someone who has recently been widowed may need practical help in dealing with financial matters if her partner used to take all the responsibility for this. She may need social support to meet new people to help with loneliness. She may need emotional support to help her come to terms with her husband's death and her feelings of loss.

You will have to work out what you can offer; it may not be possible for you to provide all the support an individual needs. However, you should be able to support her individuality and self-esteem through the conversational techniques and interpersonal skills you have learned.

Showing warmth and understanding

Care workers are often well placed to give clients social and emotional support. You can give support both verbally and through body language. However, for the support to be meaningful, it has to convey interest, warmth and sincerity.

Activity

Briefly note down what the following terms mean to you. Note down also an example of how you might express each of these qualities in a practical way, for example with friends or family members:

● interest   ● warmth   ● sincerity   ● acceptance   ● understanding.

People have different ways of demonstrating these qualities, but you probably covered some of the following points:

● Showing **interest** means demonstrating, through words or body language, that you genuinely care about what someone else is saying. If you read the dialogue between Donna and Harry on page 6 you will have seen how Donna showed real interest in Harry by focusing on his hobby of hill-walking.

● **Warmth** is when you are able to share your good feelings about someone. You probably know people who are warm – they will smile and look directly at you and make you feel comfortable and relaxed. You can indicate warmth by an open, smiling face, a touch or gesture and by showing a genuine desire to be with someone.

● Being **sincere** means being honest and true to yourself. It does not mean pretending to agree with someone when you don't really agree, or doing something which comes unnaturally. If, for example, you find it difficult to show physical affection, but someone has told you as a carer that you should hug people, your attempts to show affection will not be genuine. The person who receives your forced affection may feel confused if he/she senses that you feel uncomfortable.

● **Acceptance** means acknowledging other people for what they are – not trying to change them or make judgements about them or their behaviour. You can show acceptance by letting people know that your liking for them is not conditional on the way they behave.

● **Understanding** is being able to show that you know how someone else is feeling. Being able to share someone's feelings is also called **empathy.** You can show understanding by your looks and words which indicate that you not only sympathise with their situation, but you also have a clear idea of what they are going through.

Supportive behaviour includes all these qualities. It means listening to what people have to say without being judgmental and without imposing your own views. It means being honest and not patronising. It means being there when the other person needs you rather than deciding that 'this is the time for a chat'. It also means letting the other person know that you have an idea what he/she is going through and that even if you don't understand completely, you will make the effort to try to do so.

This is exactly the sort of behaviour that friends expect to give and receive from each other.

Read through the following scenarios. For each one, identify the needs of the person and say what a carer could do to convey interest, warmth and sincerity – in other words, to be supportive.

1 **Mr Henderson, a man with some loss of hearing, is approaching the first anniversary of his wife's death. You know it is already affecting him.**

2 **A group of people with learning disabilities who meet at a day centre want to organise a trip to the seaside.**

Here are our suggestions:

1 Mr Henderson may need special warmth and support to help him through this painful time. A carer would encourage him to talk about his feelings and about his life with his wife. On the actual day, carers would need to be aware of its significance to Mr Henderson. They would need to be ready to talk, if he wanted to. Because of his **hearing impairment**, it would be important for all carers to speak clearly and slowly and look at him when talking.

2 The group of people wanting to organise a trip to the seaside may need several kinds of support, including organisational, practical and emotional. A carer might need to help them choose a suitable destination, find out about the cost of hiring a coach and work out how much it will cost each person. The carer would need to appreciate the balance between giving support and taking control, which he/she would need to avoid at all costs. Carers may need to help especially with any difficulties that arise, for example from individuals and organisations who put up barriers to the plans made by the group.

There are no rules about how and when you can show interest, warmth and sincerity. Like many aspects of caring – and relationships in general – you develop your skills through experience and by being open and sensitive to the needs of others.

Project

Supporting individuals

Working with someone else in your group, try to prepare a list of points about all the kinds of support a carer would

try to offer the different types of client listed below.
- Mary, an old lady living alone who will need to go into a home soon because she can no longer cope on her own.
- Jotinda, a young girl who has been ill and missed a lot of school. She is feeling very isolated and worried about her future.
- Ray, a man in his twenties who has recently come out of prison and is trying to get a job but not having much luck.

When you have drawn up your list, then video yourselves role-playing a situation where you are trying to support one of these clients. One of you should act as the client and the other as the carer. Review the video and think about how you behaved. Consider your body language, your listening and questioning techniques and the ways in which you respected the other person's individuality.

If you don't have access to a video, ask another person, preferably your teacher or trainer, to watch both of you as you act out the situation and then give you feedback. Write an evaluation of your own performance, saying what you might do differently next time. How did your partner find the discussion? Did he/she feel supported and listened to? If not, what would have improved the experience?

Working in and with groups

So far you have looked at ways of demonstrating supporting behaviour on an individual or one-to-one basis. There are many situations where you have to communicate and support people as part of a group.

Most individuals are part of one or more groups, and all groups are made up of individuals. Groups tend to take on a 'group identity' which depends on the purpose of the group as well as on the personalities of the people in the group. This is what makes the group unique, in the same way as your identity makes you unique.

Activity

Think of a group of which you are a part: your family, a club, religious group, study group, etc. First of all, describe briefly the individuals in the group, then say what you think is the group's overall identity.

Now try to think of a group of people in a care context. Think for example of a group of people in a nursing home or on a hospital ward, whether you have spent time there as a patient or helper.

Despite the variety of individuals within groups, most people within a group share characteristics or experiences that help make up the group's identity. The identity of a church group may be determined by a common experience of worship; the identity of a club may be that all the members love birds or flowers, ponies or computers.

Families may be groups of people who live together and provide love and support for each other; some families may have strict rules while others are more relaxed and democratic.

A group of people in a home for the elderly may seem to have little in common other than their age, but there may be smaller groups within the home who meet to share interests, such as playing cards, exercising or painting.

Communication in groups

Because groups are made up of individuals, communication ought to happen in the same ways as it does between individuals. However, because there are several people in a group, communication can become less organised and difficult to handle. Several sorts of communication problems can occur:

- One or two individuals dominate group discussion.
- Other people feel shy or nervous of contributing to the group.
- Groups divide into opposing camps that set up fixed positions.
- Individuals may feel threatened by the rest of the group especially if they are feeling vulnerable.
- Individuals pursue their own private conversations within groups.
- Individuals become heated or emotional and let their emotions disrupt the group.

Taking turns

One way of ensuring that everyone has a chance to contribute to a group is by giving everyone a chance to speak. The following activity looks at one way of organising turn-taking.

Activity

The next time you are involved in a group discussion, for example in a study group discussion, try the following technique for turn-taking.

One person starts speaking and holds an object, such as a stone. When he/she has finished speaking, the stone is handed to the person to the left. It is then that person's turn to speak. People may speak only when holding the stone. The stone continues to be passed clockwise round the group. People don't have to speak when it is their turn; if they don't want to, they should pass the stone on. While someone is holding the stone, no one else may utter a sound: no sighs, groans or laughter!

Explain this procedure to the group and then conduct your discussion. Ideally you should repeat the exercise a number of times with the same group so that its members become accustomed to carrying out discussions in this way.

Write down what happened when you used this technique, thinking particularly about how you (and others) listened and responded to the speaker(s).

Some group members may have found this technique awkward or embarrassing, especially at first. Usually, though, this technique allows a discussion to become more even, with people beginning to listen to each other more carefully. It is a very good way of valuing every contribution which is made and of ensuring that everyone has a chance to contribute. People should feel supported, listened to and respected.

You don't have to have a stone or other object to ensure that everyone has a chance to speak. If all the group members are aware of the importance of respecting each individual in the group, they will automatically make space for everyone to contribute.

Showing supportive behaviour in groups

This unit has looked at many techniques you can use for supporting individuals. Showing supporting behaviour in groups is based on the same techniques. In the next activity you explore how to use them in groups.

Activity

Here are a number of techniques for showing supporting behaviour, many of which you have investigated in this unit. Think of a recent group discussion or meeting that you were part of, for example a study group lesson or club meeting. How did you, or other people, use these techniques to support individuals within the group? Or if nobody did, how *could* they have used them?

- active listening, using reflection, paraphrasing or interpreting
- non-verbal communication
- questioning techniques
- showing respect for the individuality of people within the group.

You may have found it hard to think of examples of these techniques being used. This may be because it is easy, in groups, to switch off and not take an active part when other people are speaking or taking a lead. We may not consciously use our communication skills, because there appears to be less need to do so.

Some forms of communication are particularly important in groups, for example body language. This may be for different reasons.

- Only one person should be speaking at one time. If other people want to communicate at the same time, they can use non-verbal means.
- In a group of people with hearing or **visual impairment**, some members may find it very difficult to follow who is saying what. Non-verbal communication can provide an excellent signpost.
- People who feel vulnerable in a group may show their feelings through body language, giving other group members the chance to support them.

Respecting individuals within groups

Groups have their own dynamics and even can develop their own 'personalities'. For this reason people's sense of individuality may be less pronounced in a group setting. It is clearly harder to relate to people as individuals in a group of several people.

However, there are lots of ways that you can make a point of respecting people's individuality within groups:

- learning and using people's names
- finding out about the person and their ideas, opinions and beliefs
- asking them about their preferences.

Taking the trouble to get to know people will help you to communicate with them effectively, not only inside the group, but also outside it.

2.1, 2.2 C **G** **Project**

This project will help you see how groups can work together to provide support for members.

Stage 1
Gather together a small group of people you know for a group discussion and choose a topic to discuss, preferably one in which all group members are interested. If possible, ensure a real mix of people in the group. Working together, draw up a set of rules for group discussions, for example possible rules for turn-taking, who will lead it, how long meetings will be, etc. Make sure you agree these matters as a group.

Stage 2

Draw up a checklist for good group discussions based on the rules you have agreed. You are aiming to find out how well the members of the group feel they were supported in the discussion. Your checklist should cover the range of methods of support: eye contact, posture, active listening, questioning techniques, etc. The questionnaire should ask people to rate how well they were supported by each method.

Stage 3

If possible, arrange to video your discussion. Appoint a timekeeper/observer and discuss your topic for ten minutes. The observer should then report back on what he/she noticed about the discussion before opening the feedback session to the group.

- How did people feel?
- Were contributions heard and valued?
- How well did group members follow the rules?
- Were people supportive of one another?

Make any changes to your discussion rules which are necessary to ensure that everyone is given equal support and respect.

Stage 4

Pass out your checklist sheets to be completed by each member of the group.

Stage 5

Write a report summarising how well the group worked and analysing how successful different ways of support were. Show this to your fellow students and discuss how they would have dealt with any problems that arose, for example certain people talking too much, others not talking at all.

Summary

In this unit you have learned about the importance of various conversational techniques and listening skills. These will be very useful in helping you get to know and show interest in people you care for.

You have also thought about how you can help people to value themselves and improve their self-esteem. Dealing with people as individuals means recognising that they are unique, with their own particular appearance, culture, physical and mental abilities, likes and dislikes. Understanding these individual parts of someone's personality helps you to respond to that person's needs more effectively.

You now appreciate that supporting other people is an *active* process. It involves active listening and positive efforts to communicate, as well as doing more practical things – from making cups of tea to helping in the garden. We can show support by identifying other people's needs and interests and asking about them. Just to feel that someone has shown an interest can help other people feel valued.

Finally you looked at how people's needs may change when they are in groups. You examined ways of supporting individuals in group situations.

Now that you have completed the activities and projects in this unit you should be better equipped to offer support to other people – whether they are friends, relatives or clients. We hope you also understand more about yourself and the way you relate to other people. This will not only make you an effective care professional, if that is what you choose to do – it will help you in all your personal relationships.

Review activity

You have completed your work on this unit. You should now spend some time reviewing what you have achieved.

1 Grading themes

For Level 2 GNVQs you can achieve a higher grading depending on how much initiative and independent action you take in the areas of:
- planning
- information-gathering.

Action planning:

Look over all the projects you worked on for this unit and answer the following questions:

- Did you complete detailed action plans for each project?
- How much support did you need from your teacher/tutor to complete the plans?
- Did you regularly review and update your plans?
- How successful were you in achieving your plans and targets?
- Were there any areas where you didn't achieve your plans? Why was this?
- What would you have done differently?

Information-gathering:

Look over all the projects you worked on and answer the following questions:

- Did you successfully identify the sorts of information you needed to complete projects and activities?
- Did you successfully gather the information you needed? How did you do this?
- How would you assess the quality of information you gathered? Was it:
  - useful and relevant?
  - appropriate for your needs?
  - accurate and complete?
- Were there any areas where you were not able to gather the information you needed? Why was this?
- What would you have done differently?

2 Performance criteria and range

Look at the standards for this GNVQ unit. Work through the PCs for the unit and check that you have done work that will help you meet each one. Do this by noting down the PC number against the relevant work.

Finally, check through the information given under the range.

- Do you understand everything that is listed in the range?
- Are you confident that the work you have done on projects covers the range properly?

3 Core skills review

The projects in this study unit will have given you the opportunity to demonstrate core skills. In particular, you should have covered:

- Communication, Elements 2.1, 2.2

Check back over your work to see that you have shown your skills in these areas.

Are there any other core skills you think you may have covered? Look carefully over the standards for each of the three Intermediate Level core skills units and make a note of any additional core skills you think you have covered during this study unit.

Glossary

acceptance acknowledging people for what they are

body language communication of messages, often unknowingly, through posture, gesture, expression, tone of voice and other non-verbal means

contradictory messages giving out two or more messages that say different things, for example where words suggest one emotion, but body language suggests another

conversational techniques methods used to start a discussion between two people, to continue it and to get other people to talk

culture the background in which a person grew up or lives; cultural influences include religion, language, dietary preferences, choices of clothes, social customs and habits

dependent relying on other people to provide help because someone is unable to look after him or herself in some way. Children are dependent on their parents

feedback information given to someone about how they have done something; it can be used to improve performance or to understand what has gone wrong

funnelling a conversational technique of moving from broad questions to more specific ones, to focus in on an issue or problem

hearing impairment difficulties with hearing

institutionalised when a person relies totally on the routines of the institution to meet his/her needs

interest demonstrating that you genuinely care about what someone else is saying

interpretation a conversational technique which involves identifying the deeper or hidden meaning of what someone is saying

non-verbal communication information about the way people are feeling through gestures, expressions and posture, rather than through spoken language

observer someone who gathers information through watching and listening carefully

paraphrasing a conversational technique which involves listening to someone and then summarising the main points of what has been said

reflection a conversational technique which involves listening carefully to the other speaker and repeating back what he/she said in a way which shows you have understood

self-esteem the value people place in themselves, a feeling of one's own worth

self-image the view people have of themselves which may depend both on how other people see them as well as internal feelings

sincere being honest and true to yourself

supportive behaviour helping someone by listening in a sympathetic and warm way or by some practical way

understanding the ability to show that you know how someone else is feeling

visual impairment difficulties in seeing

warmth the ability to share your good feelings with someone else

Influences on health and well-being

G
N
V
Q

Contents

LONGMAN

Introduction

When thinking about health or well-being, we are dealing with very personal aspects of our lives. 'Health' describes our individual physical condition, while 'well-being' concerns how we feel. However, health and well-being are not just individual and personal matters.

A whole government department looks after aspects of the nation's health. Many voluntary organisations and pressure groups also constantly ask us to consider aspects of health.

Other factors can also influence people's health and well-being, such as unemployment, violence, surviving a disaster. These are events that lie beyond an individual's control but which can considerably affect that individual's health.

This unit focuses on three different aspects of health and well-being:

1 social factors;
2 the effects of discrimination;
3 lifestyle factors.

By the end of this unit you should understand the enormous variety of influences that affect our health and well-being. This understanding is particularly important if you want to work in the health or care services. In these fields you will interact all the time with people who need care – whose well-being may be affected. Greater understanding will help you to offer a better level of support and care.

1

How social factors affect individuals

In this first section of Unit 2 you will look at how social factors influence individuals' well-being. The activities in this section should help you to understand what is meant not only by 'well-being' but also by 'social factors'.

Well-being

Activity

How would you define well-being? Read through the list of suggestions below and decide how important each one is. Give a rating on a scale of 1 (not important) to 5 (very important) according to how important you think each suggestion is.

Well-being means:
- feeling physically fit
- generally feeling good about yourself
- spending lots of time doing things you enjoy
- having a good relationship with your family
- having a good social life and lots of friends
- having a boyfriend or girlfriend
- having a secure, well-paid job.

What other factors affect your well-being?

All the suggestions given above *can* contribute to feelings of well-being. If we feel fit, that may make us feel relaxed and happy. We also need a certain amount of security to feel good – in relationships, in our family and with our friends. You may have noticed that many aspects of well-being are to do with the way we relate to other people. For example, we may need the security of a close relationship to boost our confidence, while a secure job gives us a position in society and increases our self-respect.

We are all constantly influencing other people and being influenced by them in turn. These external influences – the times when we interact with society – are called **social factors**. You will explore the range and scope of these factors in the next activity.

Activity

You may have identified the following influences:
- your parents or other family
- your school or college
- how much money your parents or family have
- what 'class' you come from
- who you mix or socialise with
- the community where you live.

1 What social factors have influenced your development? Brainstorm in a group, or list individually, all those factors that go towards making you who you are.

Consider, for example, your childhood, family, friends and communities in which you have lived. Write your ideas on a sheet of paper: on one side list the factors; on the other, list how they influenced you.

2 Which of the factors you listed do you think had the most influence on you?

Community

Money

School

Parents

Friends

Class

Other social factors become important at later stages of your life, such as your job, whether you start your own family, decisions you make about where and with whom you live.

Being part of a group

You have thought broadly about the way aspects of **society** influence individuals. One useful way of looking at society is in terms of **groups** – particularly the family. In many ways this is the most important group, as it influences us when we are young and still learning about life. Other groups include:

● the people we mix with at school
● leisure groups such as sports teams or music groups
● the whole community we belong to – our village, town, city, county or even country.

Activity

List all the groups you belong to. Compare and discuss your list with those of others in your study group.

How groups work

When you belong to a group you learn its rules – how to behave within the group. These rules are called **norms**. For example, in your family, norms may include the following:

HOUSE RULES

1. Every family member takes it in turn to wash up.
2. Children must seek permission from parents to go out.
3. There are certain meals when the family always sits down together.
4. The TV is switched off at mealtimes.

Children learn their family's norms at an early age in a processscalled socialisation. This means 'becoming social' – learning how to relate to other people as individuals and within groups. Youngchildren start by learning how to relate to other members of the family. Then they learn about roles they will have when they grow up, including, gender roles. These roles teach boys and girls to adopt particular attitudes and expectations according to their sex. Traditionally boys have been brought up to be the bread-winner and head of the family. Many girls are taught that they should prepare for marriage and mother-hood and put their family before a career.

55

Group norms and individual well-being

The norms in a group may be formal rules – a sports team may have
clear rules about the start and finish times for practices; a discussion
group may have rules about who can speak and for how long. Other
norms may be unwritten, relating to the overall preferences of the
group. For example when you socialise with a group of friends, you
may be expected to dress in a certain way, to like certain music and
to share similar ideas.

This set of group norms is that group's **culture**. Like 'society', the term 'culture' can be applied on a large scale, e.g. when talking about the national culture of a country, or it can be applied to much smaller groups.

In an earlier activity you listed groups you belong to. From that list, pick two groups that have very different rules or norms. For example, a formal group, with clear rules, such as a sports team or an informal social group.

1   **List the norms for each group. In what ways are they different? How are they similar?**

2   **What happens to someone who does not conform to the norms – who breaks the rules?**

People who choose not to conform to a group's norms are likely either to be punished in some way or to be rejected by the group. Punishment can take many forms:

- In a family, a child may be ordered to go straight to bed.
- In other social groups there may be emotional punishment, i.e. you are made to feel you have 'let the side down'.
- In employment, there is the risk of being overlooked for promotion, or even sacked.
- In society as a whole, breaking the rules can lead to imprisonment or to penalties and fines.

We all depend on different groups to help to maintain our well-being. If we are happy within our groups we can gain emotional and even financial fulfilment. Punishment or rejection by fellow group members can seriously affect our well-being.

Roles and status

Within every group, members have different roles and not all are equal. Some people lead, others follow. In formal groups these roles may be given names such as Chair, Secretary, Treasurer, Press Officer. In other groups the roles may be much less clear. Relationships vary – some people may seek power, the group may be quite democratic or one person may clearly dominate.

Activity

Think again about the groups you belong to and what role you play in each group.

- How does this role influence your health and well-being?
- Does it improve it or help to maintain it? If so how?

Here are two quotes which describe some people's responses to this activity.

Sita   'I am captain of the school hockey team. I love playing and I get a real buzz every time we have a match. Being captain gives me real feelings of pride and achievement. I think it also makes the younger players look up to me.'

Kevin   'My mother married my step-father two years ago – she'd been widowed ten years before. I hate having him in the house. He treats me like a child when I'm nearly sixteen. It's me who's been the man of the house and I can't stand having him pretending he is.'

Sita describes how being a member of one group — her hockey team — gives her a sense of pride and well-being. She also describes the **status** she feels she attains through being captain. Kevin, on the other hand, is in the middle of a battle about status within his family. This sort of struggle can be extremely stressful for everyone in the family, including his mother who may feel pulled in both directions.

Activity

Here are two pen portraits of people who need a lot of care.

- Rose is 90 and lives in a residential home for elderly people. Her husband died 24 years ago. They had no children, but a niece often visits. Rose's mobility is severely impaired and she spends a lot of her time either in bed or reading in the garden.

- Jim developed Parkinson's disease in his early thirties. He remains relatively active, although he spends a lot of time in hospital. He has a wife and three children. His colleagues from the print works where he used to work often visit him and invite him to their get-togethers.

From these details, list the groups Rose and Jim belong to. What roles do you think they have in each group and what is their status? How do you think this might affect their well-being?

Both Rose's and Jim's need for care limits the groups they belong to and the roles they play. For Rose, the most important groups are made up of care staff and other residents in the home. Her limited mobility makes it hard for her to be active in groups outside the home.

Jim, too, finds the range of groups he mixes with limited, although he has social and family contacts. These are extremely important and help to motivate him to fight his disease.

One role you may have listed for both Rose and Jim is that of client or patient. This role implies being more or less dependent on other people. Many people in this situation experience acute isolation, powerlessness and low self-esteem. People working in the health or care services need to be aware of this, so that they can give power back to (or **empower**) their clients.

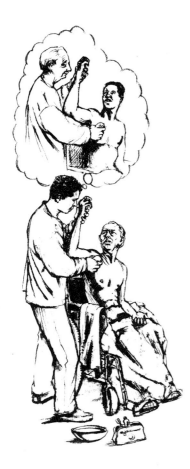

Activity

Below are listed some ways in which health and care workers can help patients/clients to cope with their dependent role. Imagine yourself as a particular health or care professional (care home assistant, hospital consultant, trainee nurse) and for each job list three things you could do to help your patients/clients in this way.

- Treat patients and clients as individuals.
- Take pains to find out their individual needs and preferences.
- Encourage clients to take a more active role in their care or treatment, where possible.
- Make clients aware of opportunities to take part in other groups.
- Give encouragement to friends and relatives to visit and/or participate in care.

All of these things are important aspects of care work and can dramatically affect the well-being of people who are forced into the role of 'patient'. Think about how *you* would like to be treated in this position.

The effects of class

There are many definitions of class, but, in simple terms, it refers to people's position within society. People may try to deny the existence of class, but it is one of the most significant groups to which we belong. British society is said to be one of the most **class conscious** in the world.

Activity

1 **Briefly note down eight factors which you would use to identify someone's class, for example, clothes or accent.**

2 **Now work with a partner to agree on the five most important factors and put them in order of importance.**

3 **As a class, discuss your lists and justify the order you have decided on.**

You probably found it difficult to agree on which factors should decide someone's class. You may have found that they tended to fall into two broad categories:

- *cultural*, including religion, background, behaviour, education etc
- *material*, including housing, clothes, money.

There have been many attempts to place people into their social classes usually according to their:

- income
- status
- skill
- education and training.

The terms upper, middle and lower or working class are traditionally used to describe someone's position in the class hierachy. There are now also many people who fall into a fourth division: the poor or underclass.

The Registrar General's six categories have had a significant influence on traditional thinking about class, but they are gradually being replaced by more recent attempts to reflect late twentieth century working patterns.

The Office of Population Censuses and Surveys (OPCS) uses ten main groups as the basis for its classification.

The Registrar General's categories

Professional
 – doctor, lawyer
Intermediate
 – teacher, nurse
Skilled non-manual
 – travel agent, typist
Skilled manual
 – electrician, hairdresser
Semi-skilled manual
 – sewing machinist,
  farm worker
Unskilled manual
 – office cleaner, labourer

Middle class, non-manual, white collar

I	Professional	doctor, lawyer, architect, accountant
II	Employers and managers	company directors and executives
III	Intermediate non-manual	teacher, nurse, journalist, farmer
IV	Junior non-manual	typist, clerk, shop assistant

Working class, manual, blue collar

V	Skilled manual	bricklayer, plumber, printer, miner
VI	Semi-skilled manual	gardener, bar tender, sewing machinist
VII	Unskilled manual	cleaner, labourer, messenger

Other groups

VIII	Retired
IX	Unoccupied
X	Other, mainly armed forces

Source: *Office of Population Censuses and Surveys*

These attempts at classification cannot tell the whole story as they are based soley on occupation and income. While these are certainly important factors in determining class, as you probably found in the last activity, other factors, such as lifestyle and family background, can be just as important.

The influence of class

Class membership influences our lives in quite definite ways. For example:

- Class can influence our expectations and aspirations.
- Class can determine the way we gain access to different aspects of society, e.g. the schools we go to, the jobs we do, the people we mix with.

Karl Marx (1818-1883) believed that ownership or the lack of it determined class. So, in a capitalist society as in Britain, the upper classes or **capitalists** own land and machinery while the workers sell their labour for wages.

Max Weber (1864-1920) felt that it was education and experience which gave people a strong or weak position in the job market and was the basis for class division rather than wealth.

Activity

In pairs or in a group, discuss the ways in which 'class' influences individuals. What do people in different classes expect? In what ways are their lives different?

Think particularly about the areas of education, health and employment. You may like to draw up a table for your answer with the different classes you have identified down the side and the different areas of influence along the top.

People with money and position may expect — and are able — to send their children to private schools. State schools provide education for people without sufficient money and for those who believe in equality of opportunity for all. Children of middle class families are more likely to go on to university and gain further qualifications than children of unskilled workers.

Private healthcare is available to those who can afford it so they do not have to wait for treatment. Babies born to parents with professional occupations are less likely to die than those born into families with unskilled jobs.

Certain jobs seem to be open only to those with a certain type of education or even from a particular school. Since children from working class backgrounds are less likely to have higher qualifications, they are less likely to be able to enter higher paid occupations.

Clearly these differences have an enormous effect on an individual's health and well-being.

2.3 AN, 2.1, 2.2, 2.3 IT **ⓒ** **Project**

In this project you will carry out some research into class. You will need to survey up to 20 people – friends, fellow students, family. Try to find out what class people think they belong to. What do they think determines class? Is their class different from or the same as their parents? What about their grandparents?

Design a questionnaire which will help you gather the information you need; you may use a word processor to produce it. You can let your subjects complete the questionnaire themselves or you may decide to interview them.

Design your questionnaire so that you can analyse your data in a mathematical way. Can you identify any trends in your data? Present the data and your conclusions in the most appropriate way, e.g. as numerical tables or as charts, graphs.

Other economic factors

Wealth is not spread evenly among the population of the UK, but is concentrated in the hands of a very few. As the table shows, 10% of the British people own over 53% of the total wealth of the country.

Concentration of wealth ownership in the UK (based on Inland Revenue statistics)

Category	% of total wealth owned
Most wealthy 1%	18
Most wealthy 5%	38
Most wealthy 10%	53
Most wealthy 25%	75
Most wealthy 50%	94
Bottom 60%	8

Source: *'Icing on the cake for the wealthy'* Labour Research April 1992

Unemployment

Unemployment or redundancy can also have severe effects on people.

Activity

How do you think the loss of a job will affect an individual? Try to think of at least three different aspects of life that will be affected.

Here are some of the things you may have thought of:
- Loss of income leads to a reduced or low standard of living.
- Social contacts through work are lost and lack of money may reduce other opportunities for socialising.
- Loss of a job can be felt as loss of status and purpose, which may lead to reduced levels of self-esteem.
- The combined effects of all these factors can cause considerable stress and depression.

Becoming unemployed is one of the most serious **adverse life-events** that anyone can experience.

Socialisation may be one important factor in explaining why men may take unemployment so badly. Most boys are taught to expect to work and to invest time and energy in their 'career'. If this fails, they may feel particularly depressed, isolated and alienated. The longer the time out of work, the worse the problem, and the older the person, the bleaker the prospect of finding new employment. In reality, however, unemployment can be just as devastating for women.

Poverty

Unemployment affects health and well-being in many ways. Unemployment may also lead to poverty, which has its own effects on health.

Death by poverty

HEALTH inequalities between the rich and the poor have been well documented for a long time ... There are large differences between rich and poor areas. For example, the lowest perinatal mortality rate for 1990–1992, 3.9 per thousand live births in Northallerton DHA, contrasts with the highest, 12.8 in East Birmingham. Another indication of the growing health divide is the rise in cases of the killer disease tuberculosis (TB) which had been steadily declining since the 1950s. *The Observer* newspaper reported that parts of London have proportionately as many TB victims as several Latin American countries.

'Death by Poverty', *Labour Research,* December 1993

Activity

The extract before gives one example of how poverty can affect health. What other ways do you think a lack of money can lead to lower levels of health and well-being? Think about particular aspects of living, such as housing or diet.

Thinking of just one area, poverty is associated with poor housing. People who live in overcrowded conditions, or properties that are damp, decaying or inadequately heated, may be vulnerable to disease. For example, children living in poor housing conditions are more prone to asthma than those in good accommodation.

Commitments

Another aspect of economics that influences people's lives is their financial **commitments**. Commitments mean longer-term obligations that you must fulfil.

Which of the following are long-term commitments?
How much of a commitment are they? Rate as: 1 = vital
commitment; 2 = important commitment; 3 = a commitment
that can be given up.

- mortgage
- car bought on hire purchase
- TV/washing machine bought on hire purchase
- private education for a child
- bank loan taken out to pay off credit card debts
- a credit card debt of £1,000
- £100 a month paid into a savings account.

You may have decided that all of these are long-term debts but some are more of a commitment than others. For example, you can stop paying into a savings scheme quite easily but if you don't pay your mortgage you may lose your house.

How individuals handle debt depends on many factors: on their personality, class expectations and their socialisation. If you come from a house-owning family that expects to borrow money to educate the children, you may feel that having a large debt is a natural part of life. If you come from a family that has always rented a house and has never owed money before, taking on a debt may be a constant worry to you.

Discrimination

Another factor influencing well-being is **discrimination.**
Discrimination – on the grounds of race, gender, age or physical characteristics – can have a devastating effect on individuals. Discrimination may be the cause of unemployment, unequal treatment by people in positions of power and long-term stress, to give just three examples. You will look at the effects of discrimination later in this unit.

Lifestyle patterns

So far in this unit you have thought a lot about how external, social factors influence people. Of course, everyone can make some individual choices about how they lead their lives.

Think about each of the following areas:

1 What do you do in your spare time – what are your interests, hobbies or leisure activities?

2 How important do you think it is to be in a relationship with a boyfriend or girlfriend?

3 How important is it to you to be able to buy things, such as new clothes, a season ticket to watch a football team, entry fees to the swimming pool, etc?

All these things come under the heading 'lifestyle' and relate to three important parts of our feeling of well-being:

1 Leisure activities – e.g. 'I think of myself as a keen snooker player/aerobics expert/pigeon fancier/singer. I look forward to the time I spend on it.'

2 Relationships – e.g. 'I enjoy having a partner, feeling that I am 'special' to someone who is equally 'special' to me.'

3 Consumer behaviour – e.g. 'Money makes the world go round. It's only when you don't have money that you realise how much of life depends on it – not just the big things, like buying a house, but the little things, like buying a round at the pub.'

Lifestyle patterns involve making choices but all choices may not necessarily be 'healthy' ones. Choosing an active leisure activity, such as swimming, benefits your health and well-being. On the other hand, taking drugs or smoking 30 cigarettes a day are decisions whose effects are far from healthy.

A summary of things that influence our well-being

In this section the author has listed a number of factors that can influence well-being, and particularly mental well-being:

- age
- social class
- experience of unemployment
- personal activity level
- ethnic grouping
- marital status
- intelligence
- education
- lifestyle choices, e.g. alcohol, drugs, smoking, food.

- sex
- work commitments
- income
- personal vulnerability to stress
- personality
- employment orientation (career)
- overall physical health
- religion

Activity

1 Identify which of the items in the list are social factors and which are more to do with the individual.

2 Then decide which items you feel have the greatest influence on your own life. Number them in order of priority. You may prefer to work in pairs and interview each other about which factors have the greatest influence on you.

You have now analysed a number of social factors which influence health and well-being, including socialisation, group membership, class and culture. The remainder of this unit looks at other important factors:

- the effects of discrimination
- lifestyle factors which influence health in social settings.

2.4 C, 2.1 AN © ### Project

In an earlier project, you investigated class and trends across generations. For this project, look more closely at the experiences of three people from different generations – this could be yourself, one of your parents and a grandparent. The aim of the project is to identify how different social factors have influenced these three people at different times, e.g. during war time, during national prosperity, during recessionary times. Plan how to carry out the investigation, e.g. whether to use interviews, questionnaires or both, what questions to ask, and so on. Note down what you decide as part of your action planning for assessment.

You should investigate all the factors in the range — social, economic and lifestyle. Decide what would be the most suitable way to present the project in order to combine the personal experience of your subjects with your more impersonal analysis. For example, you may decide to include lively case studies, but you could also include analysis of statistics, such as changes in income or the cost of living.

2 Promoting equality

Section 1 showed how important social factors are in influencing our health and well-being. If we feel secure in a stable family, with a circle of friends, we can feel good about ourselves and our future.

However, life in society may not be so comfortable. Some people have to cope with particular negative pressures, of which discrimination is one of the most destructive.

In this section of Unit 2 you will consider what it means to suffer discrimination, what its effects are and how workers in the health and care sector can fight discrimination and promote equality.

What is discrimination?

It is very hard to admit to being prejudiced but to some extent everyone is. We all have irrational fears or attitudes that can lead to prejudice. It is human nature to be suspicious of things we don't fully understand. The real challenge is how we deal with these suspicions and prejudices. Discrimination only occurs when people with prejudiced attitudes *take action* that negatively affects other people. Not everyone translates their prejudices into discrimination – some people confront their prejudices and seek greater understanding.

Why are people discriminated against?

Discrimination depends on power: it is only when someone has the power to influence another person's life that they can act in a discriminatory way.

Activity

Imagine you enter a room full of people, such as a dentist's waiting room. You see the following people:

A John, a middle-aged black man

B Graham, a middle-aged white man

C Anne, a white woman in her thirties with two young children

D Arthur, an elderly white man looking shabbily dressed

E Sinead, a young woman in a wheelchair

F Darren, a smartly dressed white man in his twenties.

Before reading on, decide which of these people may have suffered discrimination and why? What sorts of discrimination do you think they may have suffered?

You may well have decided that all of these people except **B** and **F** may have suffered discrimination:

- As a black man in a predominantly white society, John has often felt treated as a second-class citizen in all aspects of life. He and his family have also suffered abuse and violence from white people.

- As a woman, Anne has experienced discrimination in different ways, including being overlooked for promotion at work in favour of men and being subjected to sexual harassment at work.

- As a man in his eighties, Arthur feels that he is no longer considered a 'worthwhile or valuable' person. He has suffered bad health and has felt as if the doctors didn't consider him worth spending time and money on.

- As someone with a physical disability, Sinead has experienced psychological discrimination in being treated as an idiot; she has also found it difficult to gain physical access to certain places she wants to go.

In each case the discrimination stems from a perception that the person concerned is in some way 'different'.

Activity

Now imagine you are given the following information about the people in the dentist's waiting room.

B Graham, the middle-aged white man is deaf

F Darren, the young white man, is gay.

Reconsider whether either of them may have been discriminated against.

In fact, they both have. Graham has had to cope with the disadvantages of a society that caters mainly for hearing people, while Darren has experienced discrimination in many forms, including physical and verbal abuse.

In both Graham's and Darren's cases, however, the basis for their negative treatment is hidden. Often, the level of discrimination is linked to how *visibly different* people are – people who are visibly very different from the majority, e.g. black people in a predominantly white Britain suffer the most widespread discrimination.

Activity

In pairs, discuss the following questions:

1 **In what ways are you different from each other? Identify three areas where you would say you are different – for example, racial or cultural origin, language, the music you like.**

2 **Each person in the pair has to find out three things about the other person. For example, if one difference is cultural origin, each person must tell the other something about their culture that he/she thinks is interesting, valuable or important.**

3 **If possible, get back into a larger group. Each person should report the three interesting things they have learned about the other person.**

This activity should have shown you that understanding the differences between people can bring about a positive result. Getting to know people from different backgrounds and cultures should be an enriching experience.

People who *fear* difference may create **stereotypes** — building up a two-dimensional picture of people and assuming that all people fit into that model. Stereotyping denies individuality. For people working in health and care, respecting individuality is a fundamental principle of the caring process. For this reason, there can be no place for stereotypes, prejudice and discrimination. By its very nature, caring for people should mean promoting individuality and equality.

The next part of this unit looks at four areas where discrimination produces particularly negative effects:

Racial discrimination

Racism is discrimination directed towards people belonging to minority ethnic communities – that is social groups who have an ethnic origin, culture, language or religion that is different from the majority of the population.

People who are black or of Asian origin are often targets of discrimination in Britain because their skin colour is a visible focus, but not all ethnic minorities in Britain are black. Irish people, Greek and Turkish Cypriots, refugees from the former Yugoslavia, Jewish people – all may suffer discrimination. In their cases, it may be their language or culture that forms the target for discrimination.

Activity

Imagine talking to people of the following origins now living in Britain. Which of them would you regard as being from an ethnic minority group?

Polish	French	Bangladeshi	Jamaican	Irish	Scottish
Cornish	Italian	Rumanian	Swedish	Cypriot	Australian

Which of these groups are most liable to suffer discrimination?

Some people would argue that all of these groups are ethnic minorities. They would say that there are aspects of being Scottish or Cornish that make these people 'different' from the majority population in Britain. This highlights the absurdity of focusing on 'different-ness', when the similarities that exist between people of all ethnic origins and cultures far outweigh the differences. However, when people focus on obvious or visible differences, such as skin colour, that is when discrimination can be most serious. This is why people of Bangladeshi or Jamaican origin are most at risk from discrimination.

Effects of racial discrimination

People from ethnic minority groups suffer discrimination on all levels, from verbal abuse to physical violence. In employment, it may mean unfair treatment, lower levels of pay, being overlooked for promotion, being denied certain kinds of job or not being recruited in the first place.

Only joking – some of my best friends are black!

Source: *Agenda*, the journal of the National Council for Civil Liberties, November 1993

- 20% of all housing accommodation agencies are guilty of discrimination
- Ethnic minority groups experience unemployment at twice the rate of white people.
- only six per cent of barristers and less than two per cent of solicitors are from ethnic minorities.'

Sex discrimination

Sex discrimination is based on a person's gender. Even though women form over half the population of Britain, it is largely men who hold power and who use it to discriminate against women in all areas of life.

> '75 years after the suffragettes won the vote, women do
>
> 75 % of the lowest paid jobs and earn less than
>
> 75p for every pound earned by a man
>
> 75 % of single parents live in poverty, and over
>
> 75 % of part-time workers have no holiday pay, no sick pay, no maternity leave.'
>
> Source: *Agenda*, the journal of the National Council for Civil Liberties, February 1994

This quote shows how far many women are from equality. It also shows how discrimination leads to a vicious circle of disadvantage and poverty. However, in March 1994 the House of Lords ruled that part-time workers (the majority of whom are women) should have the same rights as full-time workers. Some of the ways in which women experience discrimination are outlined below.

Employment:
- being paid less for doing the same job
- being overlooked for promotion
- being given less prestigious jobs
- not being taken seriously or being patronised.

Education:
- not being encouraged to go on to higher education
- being channelled into 'feminine' specialities.

General social:
- being exposed to verbal and physical harassment
- being pressured into accepting domesticity (by parents, society, men), rather than pursuing careers.

Ageism

Many people find that they are discriminated against on account of their age. This sort of discrimination may be directed towards young people but is more usually aimed at older people. A term often used to describe this is **ageism**.

Assumptions about older people

As with other forms of discrimination, ageism stems from prejudice and stereo-typed assumptions about older people.

> **Activity**
>
> **Imagine you are starting some voluntary work in a residential home for elderly people. You ask your new supervisor to describe the residents. Which of the following terms would you expect to hear?**
>
> | | | | | |
> |---|---|---|---|---|
> | good looking | fit | healthy | lonely | sexy |
> | glamorous | powerful | influential | frail | confused |
> | ignored | senile | dependent | active | fun |

All too often descriptions of older people focus on negative aspects of being old: confused, dependent, senile, frail. When positive descriptions are used, they are often given with an implied 'for his or her age', e.g. 'He is very active (for his age ...)'. Some descriptions are almost never used for older people, such as 'sexy' – most people would be shocked to hear this description being used about an older person.

We are all conditioned to see old age as a time of potential problems, of failing health and of dependence on other people.

Older people may experience loss of power in many ways. They may lose financial power and status when they give up work. If their physical or mental health deteriorates, they may become dependent on their family or care professionals – and people who are dependent on others are also more vulnerable to discrimination.

Discrimination against older people can take the form of physical abuse, including isolated attacks by strangers, as well as regular abuse by family or carers. More subtle forms of discrimination include having their opinions and needs ignored, or being lumped together with other older people.

People with disabilities

Another reason why people are discriminated against is because they have a disability. Disability can take many forms and be more or less severe. People may be disabled physically or have learning disabilities – or they may be challenged in both ways.

Activity

Below are listed some disabilities that people may have. Work through the list and decide whether each item is a physical disability, a learning disability or a combination of both.

- Down's syndrome
- motor neurone disease
- permanent paralysis from the waist down
- severely impaired hearing
- Parkinson's disease.

Now list up to ten more forms of disability, and decide whether each is a learning or a physical disability.

Your list should show how 'disability' can mean completely different things and present individual people with very different challenges and needs. However, disabled people often have to suffer the same stereotyping as other groups facing discrimination. Ways in which able-bodied people make assumptions include:

- assuming that physical disability means mental disability
- addressing remarks to carers or other people, rather than talking to the person directly
- unwelcome interference, e.g. assuming that a disabled person needs help without asking first.

This sort of behaviour can lead to different forms of discrimination and abuse:

Verbal harassment:
- asking intimate questions about a person's disability, for no medical or other good reason
- using offensive language
- name-calling, taunts, jokes, mockery
- making the assumption that disabled people don't have a social, private or sexual life.

Physical harassment:
- uninvited touching
- patting on the head
- physical abuse or intimidation
- sexual abuse or harassment.

Another very obvious form of discrimination is found in the lack of physical access to public places. It is largely able-bodied people who design and plan buildings – all too often the needs of disabled people are overlooked.

The challenge for care workers is to treat everybody as an individual and to respond to their individual needs as people, not to respond solely to their disability.

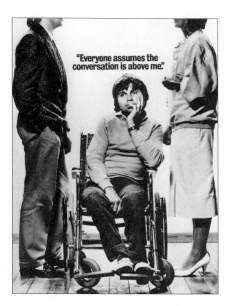

Forms of discrimination

You have now thought about the many reasons why people are discriminated against.

Activity

Consider the following scenarios.

1   Male doctor to patient: 'You're the fourth single mother we've had in this week. You really should be more careful. A life on social security is no fun, you know – though I expect the council will move you to the top of the housing queue now.'

2   Newspaper report: 'A 25-year old health care assistant was attacked in the waiting room of a local hospital. The woman, who is of Asian origin, had her face slashed by the two white men, who shouted abuse at her.'

3 Worker to Asian patient, called Shakuntala: 'Your name's a real mouthful! You won't mind if I just call you Shaz, will you?'

4 Worker at a day centre for the elderly, talking to a black man: 'There are a couple of... er... people you'll like over there. (pointing to two other black people in the corner). Why don't you go over and talk to them?

In what ways are each of these people being discriminated against?

As these examples show, discrimination can take many forms:
- verbal abuse (**2** and **3**)
- physical abuse (**2**)
- being excluded, e.g. from employment, education or social contact (**4**)
- having opinions and beliefs devalued (**1** and **3**)
- being judged according to stereotypes rather than as an individual (**1**)

What does it feel like to be discriminated against?

Activity

Put yourself in the position of any of the people in the last activity who were discriminated against? How do you think they felt?

Quite apart from the pain of physical violence, discrimination can cause severe anxiety and stress and even lead to mental breakdown. One health services trade union carried out a survey on sexual harassment suffered by its members:
- 86% of respondents said the experience adversely affected their emotional well-being
- 39% said it affected their relationships with friends and family
- 20% said it affected their health.

Quotes from people who responded to the survey:
'It made me feel worthless, ashamed.'
'It affected my sleep, worrying why I didn't have the courage to report him.'
'This incident happened thirteen years ago and it still makes me hurt and angry to recall it.'

Victims of discrimination sometimes become convinced that they are responsible for their own persecution and ask: 'Is there something wrong with me? Is it my fault?' Added to this are the financial effects of discrimination. When people are denied access to better jobs, good jobs or any job at all, they are also financially disadvantaged.

Preventing discrimination

Preventing and fighting discrimination is something everyone can do.

You can take steps in many ways:
- on a personal level
- in your interaction with other people
- on an institutional or organisational level.

Some of the most important steps are to:
- identify discrimination – in all its forms
- challenge anyone who acts in a discriminatory way
- examine your own beliefs – identify any prejudices you hold
- examine your actions – do you act in a discriminatory way?
- examine the policies and practices of an organisation
- join a campaigning or support organisation.

For health and care workers, all these steps are especially important as the people they care for may be vulnerable or have particular, individual needs.

2.2 C **C** **Project**

For this project you will investigate the experience of one group of people who suffer discrimination, i.e. older people. You should produce a report that explains:
- Why older people are discriminated against.
- What forms this discrimination takes.
- How it affects people individually and as a group.
- How discrimination can be prevented.

There are a number of ways of approaching this project:

1 **Investigate stereotypes: Collect examples of how people in your chosen group are stereotyped in the media. This could be in advertisements, in articles or portrayals on TV and radio. What sorts of stereotypes are portrayed there? Can you identify different themes?**

2 **The effects of discrimination: Arrange to talk to older people to discuss the issues mentioned above. You could talk to friends or relatives or to people living in a home for the elderly.**

3 **Preventing discrimination: Draw up a 'Clients' Charter', stating what rights clients in a home for the elderly should enjoy. Give guidance for care workers about how to avoid discrimination.**

3

A healthy lifestyle

This section looks at the wider aspects of our lifestyle – and their effects on health and well-being. These factors include: diet, exercise and personal hygiene as well as some common risks to health, including drinking, smoking, drugs and unsafe sex.

Risks to health

Section 1 looked at how our development, attitudes and beliefs are influenced by other people in our family, school and other groups. Some influences can encourage us to take up potentially harmful activities.

1 pint – nicely relaxed

2 – Very relaxed

3 – Feeling dizzy

4 – Feeling sick

5 – Feeling stupid

6 – Drunk driver kills four

Drinking

People drink because they enjoy it. In moderation, alcohol is pleasantly relaxing. Some medical experts claim that a small quantity of alcohol every day is actually good for you.

However, there are more complex reasons to explain why people drink. Social pressures are very important: drinking forms the basis of much social activity – at parties and in pubs for example. Within your peer group there may be pressures to drink if it is seen as an 'adult' thing to do.

Drinking becomes a problem when the negative effects of it start to outweigh the positive. Negative effects include:

- getting drunk, leading to loss of self-control, vomiting, hangovers, headaches
- regular drinking, leading to dependency and increasing levels of drinking
- being drunk or hungover may affect your work and even result in dismissal from your job
- physical damage, such as liver disease, stomach disorders, gout and poor skin
- depression — alcohol is actually a depressant, even though it may appear to be a stimulant
- danger of accidents, most notably when people drink and drive, but including less serious accidents such as falls
- damage to the development of the foetus by women who drink heavily during pregnancy.

1 Collect examples of any material that explains the risks of drinking to you and your peer group. Is such material readily available? Does the message come across well? How could it be improved?

2 Decide how you think the risks of drinking could be communicated most effectively to your peer group. Design whatever piece of literature you think would be most suitable, e.g. a poster, leaflet, booklet.

Smoking

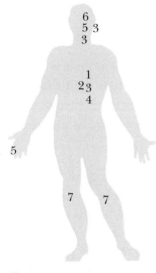

Key
1 Heart attack
2 Bronchitis
3 Cancer
4 Emphysema
5 Stains
6 Smell
7 Bad circulation – amputation

As with drinking, people usually start smoking because of social or peer group pressure. Again, there is a belief that it is somehow 'adult' to smoke. People who smoke say they enjoy its relaxing effects. Other people claim it helps them during times of stress or anxiety.

However, the adverse effects of smoking can be quite dramatic:

- Smoking causes cancer – of the lungs, mouth, tongue, nose and throat.
- Smoking increases the risk of heart attacks.
- Smoking increases the risk of chest infections, including bronchitis and emphysema.
- The nicotine in cigarettes thickens the blood, which causes it to clot in the arteries. In turn, this affects the circulation and, in some people, may even lead to limbs being amputated.

In addition to the health risks, smoking causes yellowing of the fingers and teeth and makes you and your clothes smell.

Passive smoking

Smoking does not just affect the person smoking, but also anyone else in the vicinity through **passive smoking.** If you smoke, therefore, you may be harming other members of your family, your colleagues, your friends and, in the care setting, your patients/clients.

'In 1992 a local authority worker won an out-of-court settlement of £15,000 for the damage to her health from colleagues smoking. Earlier a civil service worker had successfully claimed that her bouts of asthma, aggravated by passive smoking at work, could be considered industrial accidents. The Health and Safety Executive (HSE) has produced a leaflet on passive smoking at work, which recommends that smoking policies should be introduced.'

Source: *'Introducing smoking policies', Labour Research*, October 1993.

Many health and care organisations have banned smoking completely on their premises, especially in 'public' buildings, such as hospitals. In care settings which are also clients' homes, such as residential or nursing homes, the issues are more complex. You may feel that clients also have a right to choose to smoke. However, other clients have the right to be protected from the harmful effects of passive smoking.

Some places compromise by allowing clients to smoke in their rooms or in special smoking areas. Wherever smoking is allowed, it is important that clients are aware of the risks to themselves and other people. They should also be aware of the fire risk involved, e.g. from dropped cigarettes or matches. To avoid this risk, many care settings only allow supervised smoking.

Activity

1 What material do you know of that explains the risks of smoking to you and your peer group? If you can, collect examples. Is it readily available? Does it communicate the message effectively? How could it be improved? Does it give information and advice about giving up smoking?

2 Decide how you think the risks of smoking could be communicated most effectively to your peer group. Design a suitable piece of literature, e.g. a poster, leaflet, booklet. Include advice on how to give up, or avoid starting, smoking.

Sex and health

Sex is an important part of life. As well as being the way in which humans reproduce, it is a source of pleasure and fulfilment. However, while sex can promote well-being, it can also present threats to health. Knowledge of these threats and the precautions to take against them will help to ensure good health.

HIV and AIDS

HIV and AIDS were first identified in the 1980s and are now jointly recognised as one of the greatest threats to many people's health. AIDS is a worldwide problem that is proving particularly devastating in Third World countries where prevention and treatment are less developed than in western countries.

- AIDS stands for Acquired Immune Deficiency Syndrome.
- HIV stands for Human Immunodeficiency Virus.
- HIV positive (HIV+) means being infected with the HIV virus.

HIV is a virus that enters the body and may remain undetected for many years. This virus attacks the immune system and leads to the condition called AIDS. In people with AIDS, the body's immune system – its defence mechanism – begins to break down and the body becomes vulnerable to all sorts of illnesses and diseases, leading eventually to death.

Activity

Below is a list of activities. How great is the risk of passing on the HIV virus with each one?

- kissing
- penetrative sex
- a baby being breast fed
- sharing an ice cream with someone who is HIV+
- drug users sharing needles
- oral sex
- from mother to foetus, via the blood stream
- hugging
- blood transfusions

The HIV virus is only transmitted in human body fluids. These are:

- blood
- semen
- vaginal fluids
- breast milk.

The virus must enter the bloodstream to cause infection. The virus does exist in saliva but in such small quantities that experts don't regard kissing as a high-risk activity. Therefore sharing an ice cream is perfectly safe, as is hugging. All the other activities are potentially high risk ones, although oral sex is most dangerous when semen or vaginal fluid is swallowed, or if you have a cut in your mouth. Blood transfusions are potentially dangerous, but all blood and blood products used in Britain are now screened for the HIV virus, so blood transfusions should be safe.

Activity

Publicity has been given to certain groups within the population who are said to be most at risk. These include:

- gay men
- drug addicts
- anyone who has a lot of sexual partners
- prostitutes, both male and female
- people requiring blood transfusions.

1 **Why do you think these groups are thought to be most at risk?**

2 **Does that mean that people who don't fall into any of these groups are not at risk?**

3 **How would you publicise the risks of HIV and AIDS to people in your peer group?**

In recent years health education agencies have focused on the particular groups mentioned above. This has had both good and bad results. On the one hand, levels of infection are falling among groups such as gay men, who have responded positively to the challenge by practising safe sex using condoms. On the other hand, infection rates continue to rise among the heterosexual population.

Some argue that by publicising AIDS as a problem only for a few minorities, the government, media, etc., have understated the fact that it can affect anyone in the population. Worldwide, for example, AIDS affects far more straight people than gay. Emphasising the connection between AIDS and minority groups, such as gay men, has also meant that these groups have been exposed to increased prejudice and discrimination.

Other sexually transmitted diseases

HIV and AIDS have been the main focus for information about diseases that are transmitted sexually, but it is far from being the only sexually transmitted disease. Some other such diseases include:

- hepatitis
- herpes
- gonorrhoea
- thrush
- syphilis.

2.2, 2.4 C **G** **Project**

Carry out research into sexually transmitted diseases, e.g. by visiting your local doctors' surgery or health promotion unit. Find out what diseases pose the greatest risks to health, how they affect people and how they are transmitted between people. Summarise your findings in the form of a chart.

As part of your project, draw up a list of guidelines for minimising the risks of catching HIV or any other sexually transmitted disease. Think about the best way of presenting this information to your peer group.

Drug abuse

You have looked at smoking and drinking. Both alcohol and tobacco are drugs. Although they are relatively socially acceptable, they can both be harmful. There is a range of other drugs that can also be harmful.

Activity

Below is a list of different sorts of drugs. As a group, or individually, decide how harmful you think each of the drugs is. Draw a line like the one below and indicate where on the line you think each drug comes.

Harmless ←————————————————→ Hazardous

Heroin   Aspirin   Cigarettes
Sleeping pills   Glue   Gin   Ecstasy
Cannabis   Beer   Aerosol solvents

Can you think of any other drugs? Where on the line would you put them?

All the drugs listed can be extremely hazardous to health. 'Hard drugs', like heroin, LSD or cocaine, are some of the most hazardous because they very quickly lead to dependency and, if taken in large quantities, death.

Cannabis is regarded as a 'soft drug'; its effects are less dramatic in terms of the 'high' that users get from it. Some people would regard tobacco and alcohol as soft drugs.

Some of the other items listed, like glue and other solvents, aspirin and sleeping pills, become harmful when they are misused. The reason that drugs attract people is because of the excitement or thrills that they seem to offer. There may be pressure within your peer group to try certain drugs and a lot depends on how available the drugs are. But all drugs come with risks attached. These include:

- illness and disease, including heart disorders, damage to lungs, brain and other organs
- difficulty in sleeping
- HIV infection from shared needles
- accidents caused by impaired judgement
- loss of friends, family and social contacts
- psychological dependency.

With all drugs, the 'high' comes at a price that is not just emotional or social but also financial.

Some statistics:

Money spent on buying drugs in the UK (per year)	£5 billion
Value of property stolen to buy drugs (per year)	£2 billion
Amount a crack addict needs to fund habit (per year)	£70,000
Amount a heroin addict needs to fund habit (per year)	£29,200
Cost of heroin (per gramme)	£70–£80
Ecstasy (per tablet)	£15–£20

Source: *The Observer*, 27 February 1994

How to reduce the risks from drugs

- Don't take them.
- Seek professional help.
- Try to promote a culture of non-drug-taking in groups you mix with.
- Avoid mixing with groups where drug-taking is part of the group's culture.

2.3 C **C** **Project**

Think of ideas for a TV advertisement on the risks of taking drugs and/or how to reduce them. Think up some design ideas – you could even draw a story board (i.e. a series of cartoon/illustrations showing situations in the advert). What advice would you give to the TV programmers about when to show the video to achieve maximum impact

If your ideas are not too ambitious, you could even make the video, using your own or your school's/college's facilities.

Explaining risks to clients

In this section you have looked at four lifestyle risks: drinking, smoking, unsafe sex and drug-taking. You have thought about how you could explain these risks to your peer group in the most effective way. People who work in health and care often have to explain these and other risks to their patients/clients.

Activity

Working in pairs, think of one particular client group, e.g. children, young people, adults, the elderly. (Different pairs in your study group could choose different client groups.)

What would be appropriate ways of giving information and advice to each client group about health risks? What would be inappropriate? What are clients' rights in this situation?

It is important to remember that clients always have the right to say 'no' – to reject any advice or guidance you give, providing that their decision doesn't adversely affect other people. For example, a client may reject your advice about the risks of smoking, but that client must still observe the smoking policy of the care organisation, as must all other clients and staff.

A healthy diet

Every day each of us makes decisions about our choice of food that affect our health. Food provides the fuel that keeps our body's engine running smoothly. However, too little or too much food, or the wrong types of food, can lead to problems.

Activity

Who decides what you eat? Who influences you? Below is listed a range of likely influences. How important do you think each one is?

- family
- friends
- TV and other advertisements
- convenience – what is available
- your own preferences
- religious beliefs
- other beliefs (e.g. that eating meat is wrong)

Are there any other influences that are not listed here? Now think about the following client groups:

- people in the general surgery ward of a hospital
- elderly people in a nursing home
- a group of clients with learning disabilities in a day care centre.

Who do you think makes choices about their food? Who should make the choices? Put yourselves in the position of any of these clients: how would you like the decisions to be made about what you eat?

We don't always have control over our diets. Parents or partners may buy and cook food. If we are busy, we may snatch a quick snack without thinking about how healthy the food is. On the other hand, you may have quite strong reasons for your choice of food, perhaps because of religious beliefs or a belief in the sanctity of all animal life.

People who spend a lot of time in hospitals, homes or other institutions, often have little control over what they eat as choice is limited by the need to cater for a large number of patients/clients. Even so, most health and care settings realise the importance of offering clients some choice about what they eat. Anybody working in a health or care setting has to be aware of the importance of diet, both for health and as an expression of an individual's preferences and beliefs.

What is healthy eating?

Many complicated and carefully balanced diets have been produced to help people to lose (or gain) weight, or to become more energetic and healthy. However, there are some very simple guidelines for healthy eating. In general this means eating foods that are:

- low in sugar
- low in fat
- low in salt
- high in fibre
- natural, and not highly refined.

Here are some reasons why these are *good* foods:

- Sugar rots teeth: eating less sugar reduces tooth decay.
- Sugar is highly fattening.
- Food that is high in fat causes obesity, high cholesterol levels and heart disease.
- Eating less salt can lower blood pressure.
- A high-fibre diet prevents constipation and helps the bowels to work effectively.
- A high-fibre diet relieves **piles**.
- A high-fibre diet helps people to feel 'full' and not overeat.
- Highly refined foods may have had the goodness processed out of them.
- Many processed foods contain additives and preservatives that increase hyperactivity in children or cause allergic reactions in all age groups.
- Calcium (contained in cheese and milk) is thought to be important for strengthening bones.
- A healthy diet promotes a good complexion and can clear up spots.
- Many people say they have more life and vitality after changing to a healthy diet.
- A healthy diet introduces many new tasty dishes.

Activity

Pick one client group and outline some of the main ways in which diet is important to them and can help them to remain healthy. If you are working in a group, pick different client groups and ask each person to give a presentation about their ideas.

2.3 C, 2.3 IT **ⓒ** **Project**

Draw up a list of 'healthy eating' suggestions which you can circulate among your friends or fellow students. Structure it according to the five principles outlined before, For example, to increase the amount of fibre, you could suggest: 'Choose a high-bran breakfast cereal' or 'Scrub rather than peel potatoes'. Present the information in the way you think will be most appropriate and effective, bearing in mind the target audience.

To carry out this project you will have to research different sorts of food and find out which are high and low in fibre, high and low in sugar, and so on.

Exercise for good health

If food provides energy for the body's engine, then exercise is important for ensuring that its parts remain in good working order. The conveniences of modern life have reduced the opportunities for us to keep active but if we don't stay active there is a real danger of our body's parts seizing up.

Stamina, strength, suppleness

Exercise promotes three aspects of fitness: stamina, strength and suppleness – often referred to as the 'three Ss'.

Promoting fitness

Stamina	Being able to keep going without getting tired or out of breath. Improved stamina means your heart and lungs can work at a higher rate for a longer time.	*jogging* *swimming* *badminton* *aerobics*
Strength	Being able to pull, push, lift and carry.	*weight-lifting* *cycling*
Suppleness	Being able to bend, stretch, twist and turn through a full range of movement.	*swimming* *yoga*

Some activities are good for more than one aspect of fitness. For example, yoga is good for suppleness but doesn't develop stamina while swimming is probably the best all-round exercise, with the additional advantage that the joints are free from the pressure of gravity.

Benefits of exercise

Exercise has many benefits, both physical and mental. In particular, in the period after a session of exercise the body becomes less tense and more relaxed. Exercise:

- makes you feel good
- improves your self-esteem and helps to reduce anxiety
- improves your appearance by helping you to become and/or stay slim
- makes you feel more energetic
- helps you to relax and sleep soundly
- helps to make you more alert
- means you are less likely to suffer from fatigue and depression
- helps to keep you supple and more mobile as you get older
- improves co-ordination
- helps to strengthen joints and bones
- improves the staying power of muscles
- helps the heart to work more efficiently, improves the circulation and helps to protect against heart disease.

In addition to all these benefits, exercise need not cost much – you don't have to invest in a lot of expensive equipment to jog or go for brisk walks. It can also be an excellent social activity, enabling you to meet new people

Activity

1 Work through the list of benefits of exercise. Which do you think apply particularly to you? Identify one or two ways in which you could take more exercise if you think you need to. This could be a resolution to go swimming once a week, to cycle instead of driving or taking the bus. Which of the three Ss will this form of exercise improve?

2 Think about people who need care, e.g. who are recovering from an operation, are growing older, have a physical disability. How important is exercise to them? Choose one client group and work through the list, assessing how important each of the points would be for them.

In choosing activities for yourself, be realistic about what you can achieve. See if a friend or family member will join you as exercise can be more fun when shared with other people.

Personal hygiene

The final aspect of lifestyle covered in this section is hygiene. This can be a very sensitive area to talk about as it is something we regard as deeply personal.

Good personal hygiene is important:
- to keep the skin and hair in good condition
- to promote a feeling of well-being and dignity
- to make us attractive to other people
- to prevent bad breath and body odour
- to prevent infection
- to help to prevent pressure sores
- to prevent nails becoming too long or ragged.

Many of the reasons listed above are just as important for you as for any client group you might work with: keeping skin and hair in good condition, promoting a feeling of well-being, etc. However, there may be particular reasons why personal hygiene is important for some clients, e.g. to prevent pressure sores in those who are confined to bed or to prevent infection in people who are particularly vulnerable to illness or disease.

Personal hygiene, then, is more than just a question of personal preference. For health and care workers, it is vital for minimising the risk of cross-infection, i.e. transmitting illness between clients and workers.

2.2 C, 2.1 AN, 2.1, 2.2 IT ⓒ **Project**

Design a questionnaire to investigate aspects of health and lifestyle factors among your peer group. Aim to gather information about the health risks you and your peers are exposed to.

Think about what aspects of lifestyle you want to investigate, how you will pose questions, how to ensure you get accurate results, whether the questionnaire will be anonymous, etc. Use a word processor to create your questionnaire. You will also need to write a note to accompany the questionnaire, to explain what it is for, how to fill it and what to do with it.

Analyse the results of your questionnaire to identify what the greatest risks to health among your peers. If possible use a spreadsheet program to enter the data and to produce statistics. Where possible, present the statistics in graphical form, i.e. using charts or graphs.

Project

Having analysed the main risks to health, now work on a project to explain these risks to people in your peer group. You have already done some work on this: in designing literature to explain the risks of drinking and smoking and in thinking of ideas for an anti-drugs video. For this project, choose whatever is the most appropriate way of getting the message across to your peers. Alternatives include:

- a series of posters or wallcharts;
- a leaflet or short booklet;
- a display of materials you have gathered and produced;
- a presentation or seminar.

You may find it helpful to work in a pair or a small group. This will help you to cover all the aspects of health relating to this unit.

Summary

In this unit you have investigated factors that influence an individual's health and well-being. These factors range from matters over which we have little or no control, such as socialisation when we are babies, to choices and decisions we make consciously as adults about our lifestyle.

Many of the influences on us come from the society and groups in which we live. You have examined the positive benefits that can be derived from the social environment – security, well-being, self-esteem. You have also seen that society can exert negative influences such as unemployment and poverty while discrimination and prejudice can be extremely destructive in individual lives and whole communities.

The last section of this unit looked at personal choices about lifestyles. These choices can be healthy or harmful. You should now be better informed and able to make sound judgements and to influence other people in a positive way.

Throughout this section you have examined your own health and well-being and the influences that work on them. You should also have thought about issues of health and well-being for different client groups. This will help you to play a positive role in helping clients to maintain their health and well-being.

Review activity

You have now completed your work on this unit and you should spend some time reviewing what you have achieved.

1 Grading themes

For Intermediate GNVQs you can achieve a higher grading depending on how much initiative and independent action you take in the areas of:

- planning
- information gathering.

Action planning
Look over all the projects you worked on for this unit:

- Did you complete detailed action plans for each project?
- How much support did you need from your teacher/tutor to complete the plans?

- Did you review and update your plans regularly?
- How successful were you in achieving your plans and targets?
- Were there any areas where you didn't achieve your plans? Why was this?
- What would you have done differently?

Information gathering

Look over all the projects you worked on for this unit:

- Did you successfully identify the sorts of information you needed to complete projects and activities?
- Did you successfully gather the information you needed? How did you do this?
- How would you assess the quality of information you gathered?
  - useful and relevant?
  - appropriate for your needs?
  - accurate and complete?
- Were there any areas where you were not able to gather the information you needed? Why was this?
- What would you have done differently?

2 Performance criteria and range

Look at the standards for this GNVQ unit. Work through the PCs for the unit and check that you have done work that will help you to meet each one. Do this by noting down the PC number against the relevant work.

Finally, check through the information given under the range.

- Do you understand everything that is listed in the range?
- Are you confident that the work you have done on projects covers the range properly?

3 Core skills

If you have completed the projects in this unit, you should have covered the core skills listed below. You may find that you have also covered other core skills: look through the standards and decide whether there are any others which you could include in your evidence for this unit.

Application of Number 2.3, 2.1
Information Technology 2.1, 2.2, 2.3
Communication 2.2, 2.4

Glossary

adverse something that is bad or against a person's best interests

ageism prejudice and discrimination towards people on account of their age

AIDS Acquired Immune Deficiency Syndrome; a disease that attacks the body's defence mechanisms, making it vulnerable to illness and disease

class a social catagory based largely on income and occupation, to which people are said to belong

class conscious being aware of the differences between social classes

commitments·long-term obligations, especially financial, but can also refer to emotional and other commitments

culture the set of norms that a group shares, encompassing its customs, values, language, etc.

dependency on drugs, a compulsive craving; the inability to function normally without taking more of the drug

discrimination using prejudice as a basis for action, to exert a direct and negative influence on people's lives

drug any substance that has a stimulating or sedative effect on the body; often used to refer to substances that cause addiction

empower give power to; empowering patients/clients means giving them power to make decisions about their lifestyles, preferences, care, etc.

gender roles the particular roles that males and females learn to play

group a collection of individuals linked by common aims, experience or characteristics

HIV Human Immunodeficiency Virus – the virus that causes AIDS

life event an important thing that happens in a person's life

lifestyle a way of leading one's life; lifestyle choices are the decisions one makes about how to lead one's life

norms the rules that determine the behaviour of a group

passive smoking being in the same area (room, bus etc.) as a person who smokes so that you breathe in the smoke-filled air

peers people in the same broad social group; often used to refer to people of the same age group

piles (or haemorrhoids) painful, swollen veins in the anus or back passage

prejudice literally, 'pre-judging' people, i.e. making assumptions (usually negative ones) about people based on irrational fears or stereotypes

race discrimination discrimination directed towards people on account of their race, ethnic origin, culture or language

role the behaviour adopted by individuals within groups

sex discrimination discrimination directed against people (usually women) solely on account of their gender

social factors influences on an individual that are exerted by other people, groups or organisations within society

socialisation the process of learning the norms of society and groups within society

society a social community; the customs and organisation of an ordered community

stamina the ability to take exercise or perform physical or mental activities without getting tired or out or breath

status an individual's position within a group and the amount of power and influence the individual holds

STD Sexually Transmitted Disease: a disease passed on from one person to another through sexual activities

stereotype a two-dimensional picture of people based on preconceived assumptions and lack of knowledge

suppleness being able to bend, stretch, twist and turn through a full range of movement

Health emergencies

G
N
V
Q

Contents

Introduction

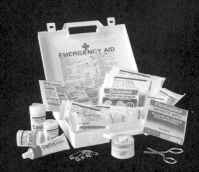

Accidents can happen to anyone at any time. Care workers are in contact with vulnerable people, such as children, elderly or disabled people, every day. When emergencies happen, being able to recognise what has happened and make decisions about what to do next could make the difference between life and death.

In this study unit, you will learn to:

- identify common emergencies
- assess the situation
- call the emergency services
- ensure your own safety and the safety of the *casualty* and others at all times.

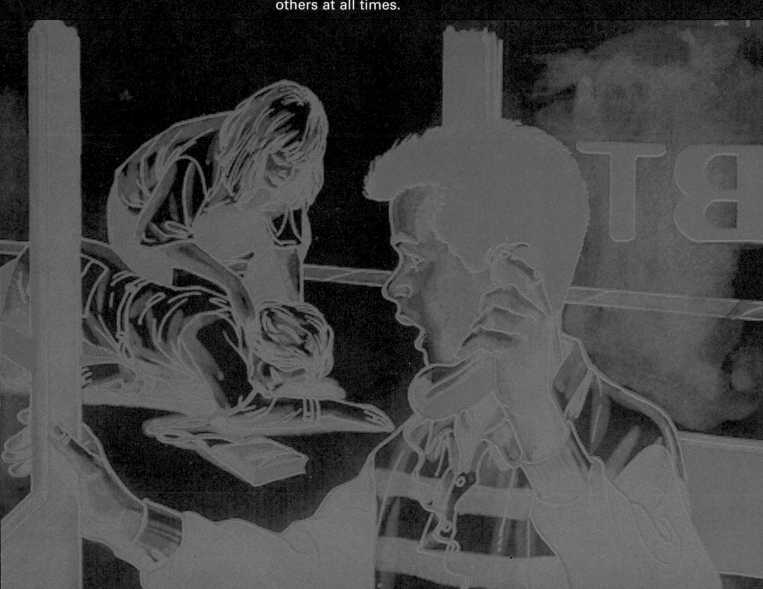

1

Identifying health emergencies

Recognising emergencies

In this first section of the study unit you will look at some common health emergences, exploring the signs and symptoms and what is happening to the body. You will also consider which groups of people may be most likely to be involved in particular health emergencies, as well as the precautions which need to be taken when attending such situations.

Activity

Have you ever had experience in dealing with an emergency? Working with a partner, take it in turns to tell each other about the situation. Consider:

- what happened
- what you think you did right
- what you would do differently next time.

It would be very surprising if you were unable to think of an emergency. Each year, over 4000 people die and over a million children have to go to hospital just as a result of accidents in the home.

Sharon saves a life

Sharon O'Shea was praised by ambulance staff for the way she saved the life of three-year-old Amanda Fortune. Seventeen-year-old Sharon had had only three lessons in first aid as part of a Caring course at her school. While baby-sitting with a friend, she went to check baby Amanda and found her lying unconscious on the bedroom floor. This is what Sharon did:

Check airway and circulation. Amanda did not seem to be breathing and had no pulse.

Action. Sharon checked for obstructions in her throat and found a crisp, which she removed. She then gave mouth-to-mouth resuscitation while her friend rang 999 for help. Amanda was breathing again by the time the ambulance arrived. Sharon says that she was nervous but had to act quickly. Could you do the same?

The following chart will help you to understand some of the most common **health emergencies**.

What happens in the body	*Signs and symptoms*

1 Asphyxia

Asphyxia or **suffocation** is when the body stops taking in oxygen. If oxygen cannot get into the blood supply, brain cells start to die after only three minutes. *The heart will stop beating and the person will die very quickly if something isn't done to help.*
Asphyxia can happen when:

- food or drink 'goes down the wrong way' and gets stuck
- someone is overcome by smoke or poisonous gas
- a person is drowning
- an **asthma** sufferer has a bad attack
- someone is crushed so that he/she can't move his/her chest to breathe
- a person's windpipe is squeezed by hanging or strangling.

- noisily gasping for air
- coughing and spluttering
- blueness or greyness of skin
- unable to speak
- rapid loss of consciousness if suffocation continues.

2 Haemorrhage

Blood travels around the body in tubes called **arteries, veins** and **capillaries.** If an artery or vein is cut, or capillaries burst, then **haemorrhaging,** or bleeding occurs. Losing a lot of blood lowers the blood pressure and can lead to shock symptoms (see 'Physiological shock'). *A major haemorrhage may result in death if not dealt with quickly.*

- bright red blood spurts out of the wound at high pressure when an artery is cut
- dark red blood may flow heavily but does not spurt when a vein is cut
- blood oozes out of ruptured capillaries caused by a punch, a blow or a fall
- a **bruise** forms when the blood remains under the (unbroken) skin.

Puncture wounds may hide deeper damage. Show them to a doctor.

3 Physiological shock

Shock is a very serious condition caused by slowing of the blood flow around the body. Oxygen does not get to the brain and other organs and the patient may die if shock is not treated quickly.

The worst risks of shock are from severe bleeding and serious burns. There is less blood available to be pumped round so the heart beats faster, but it is weaker and less effective.

Any other injury which results in a major loss of **body fluids** will have the same effect. Fractures and large bruises may also cause shock because body fluids leak inside the body or under the skin.

- changes in colour. A black person turns a dark blue/grey. White people turn a very pale grey
- cold, clammy, sweaty skin
- breathing is weak and quick
- rapid **pulse**
- strange and confused behaviour.

If you are able to recognise and treat shock, then you could save a life.

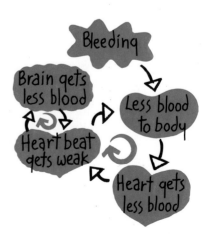

How shock develops

What happens in the body   *Signs and symptoms*

4 Heat exhaustion and heat stroke

Heat exhaustion can be the result of being out in the sun or in hot air for too long when you're not used to it. Your body overheats. Normally your body would cool itself by sweating or by warm blood coming to the surface to cool down. In very hot and humid weather the air may be as warm as your blood so sweat may not evaporate and it is difficult for your body to cool down.

of heat exhaustion
- feeling sick
- feeling dizzy
- headache
- no energy.

of heat stroke
- very high temperature (40°C or 104°F)
- red, dry skin
- **vomiting**
- bad headache
- unconsciousness (sometimes).

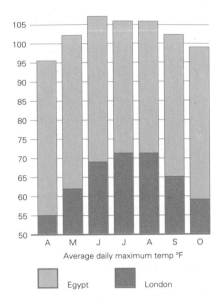

Average daily maximum temp °F

☐ Egypt   ■ London

2.1 AN **C** **Activity**

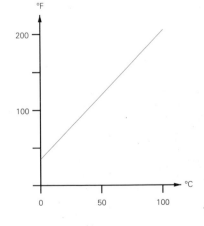

When you are dreaming of holidays, one of the most important things to consider is the weather. Holiday brochures have tables like the one above to help us decide when to travel.

Look at the table of temperatures in Egypt.
- How hot does it get in the hottest month?
- Is this cooler or hotter than your body temperature?
- What would be the dangers to your health if you visited this country in the hottest month?

You will notice that temperature can be described in both degrees centigrade (C) and degrees Fahrenheit (F). It is useful to be able to convert from one to another. Using this graph, answer the following questions:

1   **Your normal body temperature is about 37 degrees C. What is this in degrees F?**

2   **What is the temperature in Egypt in June? What is this in degrees C?**

What happens in the body　　　　　*Signs and symptoms*

5 Burns and scalds

Burns and scalds damage the skin. The seriousness of the injury depends on what area and what depth of skin is affected.

Burns are usually caused by *dry heat*, for example from a hot pan handle, friction or flames. Burns may also result from things like electric shock or sunburn. Contact with very cold things, like frozen metal, or with **caustic** chemicals, like bleach, can also burn your skin.

Scalds are caused by *wet heat*, for example steam, spilt hot drinks or getting into a very hot bath. *People who have severe burns sometimes die from shock because of loss of body fluids. By remembering this, and giving immediate treatment, you could save a life.*

Superficial burns and scalds:
- skin reddens and swells
- skin is tender

More serious injuries:
- skin may blister and feels 'raw'

Serious burns and scalds:
- skin looks pale and waxy
- area may be blackened and skin burnt away.

Superficial burns and scalds may heal well after **first aid** treatment, but *more serious burns must be seen by a doctor and may need emergency treatment.*

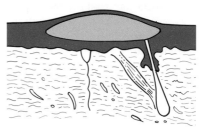

Burn blisters keep in body fluids and protect damaged skin from infection.

6 Sprains and dislocations

Sprains happen when muscles or the tissues around your joints (called **ligaments**) are injured. This can be caused by sudden twisting or stretching movements. Bones are not affected.

A more serious twist or wrench may result in bones going 'out of joint'. This is called **dislocation** and may also involve muscle or ligament injury. The most common dislocations are where joints are very flexible. Shoulders and jaws are good examples of this. Can you think of others?

Sprains, dislocations and **fractures** may have very similar symptoms. These include:
- pain at or around the injury, especially when trying to move it
- bruising, heat and swelling
- bone pushing through the skin (**compound fracture**)
- inability to move the part at all
- changes in the appearance of the affected part, e.g. its shape or direction.

Look out for signs of shock as well. *If in doubt, assume that the injury is a fracture and get the casualty to hospital.*

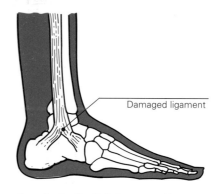

Damaged ligament

A sprained ankle. Twisting your ankle may tear ligaments

7 Fractures

Broken bones (or fractures) happen when a bone is hit hard or twisted violently. Bones are normally held in position and moved around by muscles. Broken limbs may twist and the jagged ends of broken bones may cause damage under the skin. In very serious cases, the broken bone may actually push against the skin or poke through an open wound. This would cause *severe shock*.

See 'Sprains and dislocations' for general signs and symptoms. Very bad pain, swelling and inability to move could mean dislocation or a fracture.

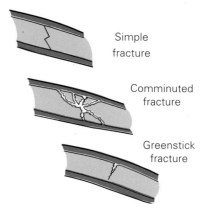

Simple fracture

Comminuted fracture

Greenstick fracture

What happens in the body   *Signs and symptoms*

8 The effects of poisons and chemicals

Poisons and chemicals can get into your body in a number of ways:
- eating or swallowing
- splashing on the skin or eyes
- by injection, or through cuts or snake bites
- breathing in fumes or vapour.

The effects of taking in poisons or chemicals might be:
- skin burns or burns in the mouth and throat
- breathing difficulties caused by inhalation
- damage to your insides as the poison gets **digested** or passes into your bloodstream.

If the casualty is conscious, he/she may be able to tell you what has happened. A common effect of poisoning is vomiting. Signs and symptoms vary according to what the poison is and how it has been swallowed. Important clues might be:
- a bottle or other container
- a smell of gas, alcohol or chemicals
- the remains of food or plants.

Minor splashes on the skin could be dealt with by first aid, but, in most other cases, professional help needs to be called quickly. *Make sure you are safe from the effects of poisons or chemicals yourself before taking action.*

Some common household poisons

9 Cardiac Arrest

Cardiac arrest occurs when the heart stops beating. The heart is the muscle which pumps blood around the body. It may stop pumping because of asphyxia (see (1) above), electric shock (see next page), losing a lot of blood or a heart attack.

The main signs of a cardiac arrest are no pulse and no breathing.

The casualty is likely to become unconscious very quickly; an ambulance must be called immediately.

10 Heart Attack

When someone has a **heart attack**, it is usually the result of a blockage, such as a blood clot, in the blood supply to the casualty's heart. The heart muscle doesn't work if blood can't get through.

Someone with a heart attack may:
- feel a dreadful pain gripping their chest
- be out of breath
- feel weak, dizzy or faint
- have bluish lips and changed skin colour (see 'Physiological shock')
- feel sick and think that they are going to die
- have a fast pulse rate that gets slower.

An ambulance must be called immediately for someone having a heart attack.

11 Stroke

A **stroke** happens when blood cannot get to part of a person's brain. An artery may be damaged or may be blocked by a blood clot. Strokes are more common in older people. The effect of a stroke depends on which part of the brain is affected.

If someone has a stroke, they might:
- suddenly feel a very bad headache
- be confused and upset
- slur their words or not be able to speak
- wet or soil themselves
- seem paralysed or weak, perhaps on one side of their body
- have one eye pupil smaller than the other one
- dribble or droop on one side of their mouth.

As with a heart attack, if someone has a stroke, you must act quickly and make sure an ambulance is called.

What happens in the body   *Signs and symptoms*

12 Angina

An attack of **angina** can occur when insufficient blood gets through to a person's heart because the arteries have become too narrow. This may happen when he/she gets excited or moves about too quickly.

Angina may be less serious than a stroke or heart attack. The casualty may know what is happening and have medicine to take. The symptoms of angina are similar to those of a heart attack, except that the chest pain may get better if the person rests. If it doesn't, then treat it as if it was a heart attack.

13 Electric shock

A mild electric shock may only make you jump. A severe one could make your heart stop beating and affect your breathing. It may also result in burns.

- the person may still be holding or touching whatever gave them the shock
- there may be burns where the electricity went into the body and, perhaps, where it came out
- breathing and heartbeat may stop. *You will need to call an ambulance if the casualty is* **unconscious** *or seriously injured.*

14 Loss of consciousness

Unconsciousness is the result of something going wrong with the brain's normal activity. An unconscious person may look as though she is asleep, but when someone loses consciousness, he/she also loses the ability to respond normally. The **reflexes** switch off. For example, he/she will not cough when his/her airway gets blocked.
Unconsciousness can be caused by:
- head injuries, which damage the brain
- a heart attack, stroke or other emergency that cuts the flow of blood to the brain
- asphyxia or poisoning (including drunkenness) that cuts the supply of oxygen to the brain.
Other causes are fainting, **epileptic attacks** or low levels of blood sugar (**hypoglycaemia**).

A person is unconscious if he/she does not respond normally. It is important to recognise the different levels of consciousness.
- An *alert* person talks and opens his/her eyes normally.
- He/she may only respond to your *voice* when you say loudly, 'Can you open your eyes?' Any response is confused.

- He/she may only respond to *pain* by moving slightly.
- He/she may be totally *unresponsive. Anyone who is unconscious for more than three minutes must go to hospital.*

The recovery position helps to prevent choking.

Activity

In pairs, look through the chart of health emergencies. Consider which emergencies are most likely to happen to children, young people and older people. Talk about why one age group is more likely than another to be involved in particular health emergencies.

The health emergencies which are most likely to occur with children are:

- suffocation and choking
- poisoning
- falls (not serious)
- burns.

Young people are most likely to be affected by:

- sprains and fractures of arms and legs
- head injuries.

The emergencies which are most likely to occur with old people are:

- falls
- burns
- poisoning
- heart attack
- stroke.

Activity

Read the following case studies. Write down:

- what you think has happened
- what signs and symptoms you expect to see
- whether or not you would call the emergency services.

Case study 1

You are queuing at the checkout at Tesco when an old lady, who is in front of you in the queue, collapses over her trolley. She is grasping at her neck and seems to find it hard to speak.

Case study 2

You are on a day trip to the seaside with the Greenfields Day Nursery children and staff. The day has been gloriously warm and sunny. You are helping to collect the buckets and spades together when Una Evans, the senior nursery nurse, collapses.

Case study 3

You are having a cup of tea in the garden with your neighbour when her youngest child, Jenny, runs from behind the shed screaming. Her skirt is in flames.

Case study 4

You are riding your bicycle home late one night when you see a car pull out and hit your school friend, Jez, who is riding his new moped. Several people have come out of the Red Lion pub by the time you've pedalled up the hill to the scene. As you approach, you notice that the car driver is bleeding and trying to get out of the car. Jez is lying on his back in the road, not moving.

Case study 5

You have been invited to watch your neighbour, Betty Copperwood, do a parachute jump to celebrate her 70th birthday. She waves joyfully from the sky, but lands badly and cannot get up.

Case study 6

You are babysitting for Holly, a lively three-year-old. You leave her playing while you answer the doorbell. The caller is a salesman and it takes a little while for you to persuade him that you don't want to buy his dusters. When you return to the kitchen, Holly is happily popping contraceptive pills from the pack she found in your bag.

Case study 7

You are playing a computer game with your friend Zeth. You turn to tell him that it's his turn and he looks at you strangely. A moment later, he falls to the floor and starts to shake violently. You notice blood dribbling from the corner of his mouth.

Case study 8

You have just started on the afternoon shift at Hillview Rest Home. A buzzer calls you to Mr Jolly's room and you arrive to find him sobbing and shaking. His trousers seem to be steaming and a mug and teapot are in pieces on the tiled floor.

Case study 9

It is the end of the morning at Greenfields Day Nursery. You are in the Quiet Room telling the children a story. You hear a crash from the playroom, where Ken Smith, the caretaker, is doing some odd jobs. When you go into the playroom, you see Ken lying on the floor. A smashed light bulb and an overturned chair are nearby. A bare wire is swinging from the ceiling.

After you have written your answers down, come together as a group. Go through the case studies one at a time and share your answers. Did you agree about when to call the emergency services?

Sometimes people decide not to call the emergency services because they are afraid of looking silly or of making a fuss about nothing. Another reason why people might not call is because they feel sure that someone else will have done it. This is especially the case if there are a lot of people about. Everyone assumes that someone else will be more expert than them.

The emergency services *don't mind* how many calls they get to the same emergency. Having read this far and done the last activity, you should have a good idea about when to call for an ambulance. Remember, 'If in doubt, call them out.'

Look back to check on signs and symptoms for each of the emergencies in the last activity.

1 The old lady might be choking (asphyxia) or she may be having a heart attack. She will need urgent first aid so an ambulance *should* be called.

2 Una may be suffering from heat exhaustion. If she does not become conscious again quickly, an ambulance *should* be called, as she could be suffering from heat stroke.

3 Jenny has been playing with matches. When her skirt caught fire, she ran for help and the wind fanned the flames making them worse. The burnt skin would be swollen and red and may be blistered. She would be suffering from shock. You *should* call an ambulance.

4 Jez may be unconscious as a result of a head injury. He may also have broken bones or be bleeding. He may have stopped breathing and have no pulse. The car driver is conscious, but he has bleeding wounds and may have fractures. Remember to look for symptoms of shock. You *must* phone for an ambulance. The police will also come to any road accident where a person is injured.

5 Betty may have sprained a joint or broken a bone in her leg or hip. If she is in too much pain to walk with support, you *should* send for an ambulance.

6 Holly may not have eaten any pills. If you know how many there were, check how many are left. If any are missing or you are unsure about how many there should be, call the doctor or take her to the hospital casualty department. Take the pill packet with you.

7 Zeth may have had an epileptic attack. If he has had one before, he probably doesn't need immediate medical help. If he has not had one before, he should see a doctor as soon as possible. If he stays unconscious for more than a few minutes, an ambulance *should* be called.

8 Mr Jolly has probably scalded his legs and will need immediate first aid. An ambulance *should* be called.

9 Ken may have had an electric shock when changing the light bulb. You must also look to see if he is conscious and whether there are signs of broken bones or bleeding from the fall. You *should* call an ambulance.

It is important to think about *how* an accident has happened, as this can give you clues about what the injuries might be.

Protecting yourself and others

It can be very frightening to be the first person at the scene of an accident, even a small one. Accidents may also be very messy and smelly. However, most people find that they can overlook unpleasantness in order to save another person's life.
We need to:
- put aside our own squeamish feelings
- try to remember what to do to stop the casualty dying
- be sure to take care of ourselves.

Some health emergencies can put the helper in danger.

Activity

In pairs, think about the situations opposite and answer these questions:
- What further danger might there be for the casualty?
- What danger might there be for you and others?
- What do you think you should do?
- What do you think you should not do?

Situation 1

As you are leaving the railway station late one Sunday night, you see a young woman clutching her head with blood-stained hands. As she vomits into a pile of rubbish by the wall, one of a nearby group of men shouts abuse at her before walking away.

Situation 2

You are leaving Greenfields Day Nursery with Ken Smith, the caretaker, after the morning session. You follow the stream of parents and toddlers down the narrow road to the town. Suddenly, a child darts off the pavement and across the road. A red motorbike swerves to miss the child and crashes into a wall on the other side of the road. The rider is thrown from the bike and it falls on top of her. It is lying across her legs with the engine still running and petrol is leaking onto the road.

Situation 3

You are on the evening shift at Hillview Nursing Home. Mr Jolly comes to tell you that he's worried about Mrs Hemingway. She has a habit of smoking in bed and there seems to be smoke coming out from under her door.

It is important in any health emergency that you *assess the situation*. Often, you can start to do this as you approach the casualty.

Here are some of the dangers that you may come up against in dealing with health emergencies:

- being hurt if you go to help someone who has been attacked
- infection from the casualty's body fluids and the risk of passing on hepatitis B or HIV
- being hurt by other traffic which hasn't had time to stop
- being burnt. Leaking petrol from a running engine could catch light
- hurting your back through using unsafe methods to lift heavy things.

You probably came up with answers similar to the following for the last activity:

1 The woman is bleeding heavily and will soon suffer from shock if she is not helped. You must call the emergency services as soon as possible. The possible dangers in this situation are:

- her attackers may return and hurt you if they see you helping
- anyone giving first aid to a bleeding casualty is in danger of possibly being infected by the casualty's blood.

2 The dangers to everyone involved are:
- other traffic causing another accident
- leaking petrol which could cause a fire. For example, if a glowing cigarette butt blew or fell near the petrol it could cause the vapour to explode.
- possible back injury from trying to lift the bike off the rider's legs.

You should:
- turn the engine off
- send someone to call the emergency services
- ask someone to warn traffic
- with Ken's help, use safe lifting techniques to lift the bike (you will learn about these in Section 3)
- move the rider to a place where she is not in danger.

3 Mrs Hemingway is in danger of asphyxiation if she is in her smoke-filled room. There is almost certainly a fire, so the alarm should be rung and a fire engine called while everyone else leaves the building. You may be in danger of asphyxiation yourself if you try to rescue Mrs Hemingway and you may spread the fire which is contained within the room by opening the door. Leave it to the emergency services.

2.1, 2.2, 2.3 C ☉ **Project**

This project will help you to draw together your work on identifying health emergencies.

Choose a particular client group in a health or care setting like Greenfields Day Nursery or Hillview Rest Home. Imagine that you had to provide information about health emergencies to the carers working with this group.

You could present the information as, for example:
- an illustrated ten-minute talk
- a set of posters
- an audio cassette
- an information leaflet.

You could include photographs and sketches.

The information should be about emergencies which are most likely to happen to the chosen client group and how to recognise what has happened. It should include an explanation of how carers can ensure their own safety.

Before you begin, write your action plan. Think about:

- what information you will need, and
- how you will find it.

Set yourself a time for collecting information and a time for preparing your presentation.

Use the information in this study unit, but remember that you will need to find other sources of evidence in order to get a _merit_ or _distinction_.

You could:

- speak to someone who works as a carer in the type of setting you are looking at and ask him/her what sort of accidents happen more often
- look for more detailed information in a first aid manual
- get information about how many people are taken to hospital for different health emergencies.

2 Dealing with emergencies

The first section of this unit looked at some of the health emergencies that can occur. By now, you will be able to recognise what might be wrong with a sick or injured person. In this section, you will consider what practical help you can offer the casualty.

Activity

Rosie Clarke is a home help. She arrived at Mrs Whittaker's flat at her usual time. She let herself in and called a cheerful 'hello' as she closed the front door. But there was no reply. She pushed open the kitchen door and, to her horror, old Mrs Whittaker was lying silent on the floor.

Rosie put a hand on the old woman's forehead and Mrs Whittaker groaned and tried to move. Rosie could see a pool of blood on the floor from an open wound on the side of Mrs Whittaker's head. Blood was also dripping from her nose.

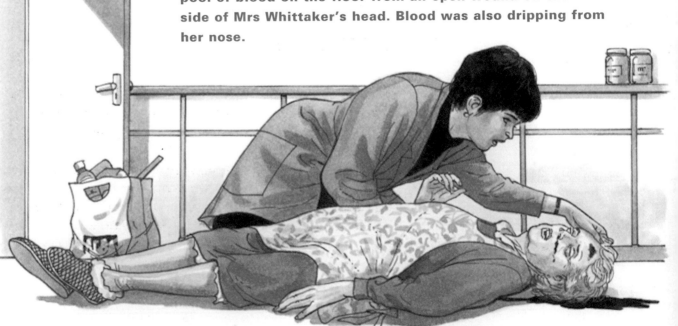

What should Rosie do next?

Re-arrange (a) to (g) into their correct order of importance

Order

(a) Put Mrs Whittaker in the **recovery position.**

(b) Check her pulse.

(c) Put on a pair of rubber gloves.

(d) Stay calm.

(e) Apply pressure to Mrs Whittaker's head wound.

(f)   Call for an ambulance.

(g) Talk to her and reassure her.

Check your answers on page 142.

Accidents are always shocking because they happen suddenly; they are often terrifying as well. In order to be of any use, Rosie would have to forget her own fear and remember that Mrs Whittaker would be much more frightened. A very important thing for Rosie to do would be to remember to *stay calm.*

   A first aider is the person who first gives help to the injured person. Often, this first aider is a family member or friend. For many minor injuries, this help is enough. However, there are times when it is necessary to call for the expert assistance of the emergency services.

Getting help

Getting help from the emergency services only needs one phone call. You don't need any money. If you don't have a telephone at home, it's a good idea to practise using a pay phone in non-emergency situations.

   If an emergency happened while you were at home, there might be more than one person available to help. In this case, one of you would stay with the injured person while the other one went for help. You must make a decision *quickly* about who should do what.

Contacting emergency services

When you ring 999, this is what happens:

- The operator will say, 'Emergency. Which service please?'
- Don't go into details. Tell him/her that you need an ambulance. If something more serious has happened, like a bad road traffic accident, then you should say, 'There has been a road traffic accident. We need all services.'
- The operator will transfer you to Ambulance Control. They will ask you the following questions.

1 What telephone number are you ringing from? Look on the 'phone or, in a public call box, the number may be on the wall facing you.
2 What is the address or the place where the casualty needs help?
3 What has happened?

2.3 IT **©** **Activity**

Everyone should know how to call the emergency services, but a set of instructions in first aid boxes or by public telephones is a useful reminder of what to do.

Using a computer, **design a poster which tells people how to call the emergency services. The poster must be** *very simple* **and** *very clear*. **Remember, the person who needs to make the call:**

- may not be able to speak English
- may be a child
- may find reading difficult.

When planning your poster, consider how to use large print, pictures and diagrams to get the message across more clearly.

How to be helpful when calling 999
- Remember to *stay calm.*
- *Answer the questions clearly and slowly*, but don't try to give the whole story.
- *Describe the place* where the emergency has happened. This may not be the place where you are 'phoning from.
- *Give landmarks* to guide the ambulance driver, for example 'The house is on the left just after the main Mobil service station as you come from Nottingham. The house has a red front door.'

• *Describe the type of emergency briefly*:

Example 1: 'My mother had a heart attack six months ago. She is having a lot of chest pain and looks very blue. I think she's having another one.'

Example 2: 'A young woman has collapsed in the loo at the college disco. She smells of alcohol and her friend says she has diabetes and needs injections for it.'

Example 3: 'A three-year-old in the day nursery has knocked a cup of freshly made tea off a table and down both her legs.'

• Put the 'phone down only when *you are sure that the controller has enough information*. This is very hard, as you will be anxious to get back to the casualty. Remember, if you do not give the correct information then it may take longer for help to reach you. Time is precious in an emergency.

2.1 C **©** **Activity**

You will need to work in a group of three people for this activity.

Each person in the group should think about an emergency situation. This might be one that you've really been in, or one that you've read about. It might even be a scene that you've watched on a TV programme like *Casualty*.

Think about what details you would need to pass on to the emergency services. Write some notes about these so that you can use them in the activity.

Decide who will be:
• the caller
• the operator
• an observer.

The caller and operator should sit back-to-back so that they can't see each other. The operator needs to find out enough information to get the emergency services to the casualty.

The caller should give the information that the operator asks for. It would be normal for the caller to be anxious and worried, so try to act the part.

After each pair has finished, the observer should give them

feedback on how they did.

- Did the operator get all the necessary information?
- How did the caller seem to feel?
- Did the caller want to give more information?

If there is time, the three people can swap places and repeat the activity until everyone has tried each role.

Golden rules of first aid

- *Try to sound calm and in control when speaking to the injured person. Don't forget that an unconscious person may be able to hear you, even though he/she can't speak to you.*

- *Don't move a casualty unless you think that he/she might be injured again by staying in the same place, for example by being run over by a car or crushed by a falling roof.*

- *Loosen any tight clothing.*

- *Keep the injured person warm. If you can manage to get a blanket underneath him/her, this will protect the person from the cold more than one on top.*

- *Do not give the injured person anything to eat or drink. The exception here is people with burns. They should be persuaded to sip water as soon as possible after the accident. They should keep sipping until they get to hospital.*

- *Don't let a crowd gather round the injured person. However, remember that bystanders may need reassuring as well, especially in a care setting like Hillview Rest Home or Greenfields Day Nursery.*

- *It's very important to watch for changes in the injured person's condition. Keep a record of this so that you can pass on the information when the emergency services arrive.*

Activity

Read this story.

Tim and Darren were going home through the park after college when they saw a group of children gathered round someone on the ground.

'It's Daljit. She fell out of the tree.'

The little girl was not moving and her eyes were closed. Darren ran off to call an ambulance. Tim took off his coat and put it over Daljit. The cord of her hood seemed very tight, so he untied it. One of the boys said, 'She was stupid.

It's Daljit. She's fallen out of the tree.

We told her not to go so high.' Tim found out that the accident had happened about five minutes before he and Darren had arrived.

He sent two of the children away to Daljit's home which was nearby. As they left, Daljit gave a little whimper and opened her eyes. Tim sent the other two children off to find Darren. 'Tell him that she's woken up,' he told them.

He thought to himself, 'She's been unconscious for about ten minutes ... must remember to tell the ambulance crew.'

He turned back to Daljit who was crying and looked frightened.

What did Tim do right in this situation? What should he have done differently? Get into pairs to discuss this.

Make two lists.

You may have noticed that Tim stayed calm and made Daljit comfortable. There was a possibility that she might have broken bones, so he was right not to move her. It was good that he noticed how long she had been unconscious. He dealt with the other children quite well and kept them busy.

Here are some of the things you might have spotted that could have been done differently:

- If he had known more about first aid, he would have checked her breathing and pulse. You can find out about this in the next section.

- He didn't realise that Daljit might be able to hear things that were being said. When Daljit woke up, none of her friends were there. No wonder she looked so frightened. You may have thought of things that he could have said to comfort her.

The equipment you need for first aid

First aid kits must be available in workplaces, schools and colleges. It is also useful to have a first aid kit at home and in the car.

Activity

Make a list of any other places you think should have first aid kits.

You may have thought that first aid kits should be kept in:

- leisure centres
- swimming pools
- libraries
- supermarkets
- cinemas
- theatres
- other places where lots of people go.

You can buy already made-up first aid kits. However, those will cost quite a lot of money and it is not difficult to make up your own kit. An ice-cream box makes a good container for first aid materials.

Activity

What do you think should go in a first aid box?

1 As a group, brainstorm what equipment you might need in a health emergency.

2 Write all your suggestions on a sheet of flipchart paper or on the blackboard.

3 Decide together which are the ten most important items.

4 List them in order of importance.

Always check first aid kits regularly. Replace anything you use as soon as possible. Missing items could cost a life.

When you've finished the activity (but not before!), look at the recommended list at the back of this study unit (page 142).

Activity

Imagine you are dealing with an emergency situation outdoors and you have no first aid kit. What could you use instead of the items you recommended in the last activity?

Possibilities for dressings for an outdoor emergency include:

- a clean handkerchief
- a clean tea towel
- any clean, non-fluffy cotton fabric.

2.2, 2.3C, 2.3 IT **C** **Project**

You have already thought about the places which ought to have first aid kits. Your task for this project is to design a questionnaire to find out about:

- where first aid materials are kept
- what the rules are about using them
- how often the contents are checked
- who is responsible for checking the contents.

1 **Use a computer to type and print out a neat copy of your questionnaire. It should be easy to fill in.**

2 **If you are working in a group, you could divide up the list of places (adding some of your own). If you are working alone, choose any two different places.**

3 **Make an appointment to visit each place and speak to someone in charge. Ask him/her to complete the questionnaire and ask if you may look at a first aid box. Make a note of the contents.**

4 **Write a report about your visit, including whether you think the first aid kit is complete. Suggest any improvements that could be made.**

Remember to prepare an action plan before you start, including details of what you are going to do and when.

Send a copy of your report, together with a letter, to the person you interviewed thanking them for their help.

Simple care procedures

By now, you will be feeling more confident about how to recognise what is happening in a health emergency. You know how to call the emergency services. You also have a good idea about what to do while waiting for the ambulance to arrive.

If the casualty is unconscious

Once you have assessed the emergency situation, the next thing you must do is to check whether the casualty is conscious.

To do this, touch him/her gently and say something like 'Can you open your eyes?' or 'Can you squeeze my hand?' Say it clearly and quite loudly.

If the casualty responds in any way, he/she is at least partly conscious and you can deal with other injuries. Put the casualty into the recovery position and get help.

If he/she is unconscious, you must move quickly on to the **ABC** of **resuscitation.**

A is for Airway

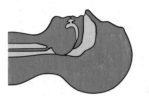

The casualty's **airway** may be blocked by loose teeth, food or vomit. Often it is the person's own tongue that has become floppy and slipped back to cover the entrance to the airway. *The casualty will die if you do not unblock the airway. You only have three minutes.*

Opening the airway
- Put one hand under the injured person's neck.
- Put your other hand on the forehead.
- Gently tilt the head backwards.
- Push the chin upwards. This should bring the tongue forwards and open the airway.
- Remove anything else in the mouth.
- Check to see whether the casualty is breathing.

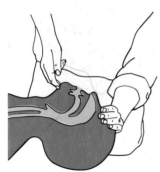

Opening the airway

B is for Breathing

To check for breathing, look to see if the casualty's chest is moving up and down. If you are unsure, put your ear close to his/her mouth and nose. Listen and feel for breath. If he/she is still not breathing, you will need to do **mouth-to-mouth resuscitation** at once.

You can find out how to do this by looking in a first aid manual, for example the St John Ambulance Authorised Manual but it would be much better to go to a class and learn how to do it on a Resusci Anne.

C is for Circulation

So far you've cleared the injured person's airway and given mouth-to-mouth resuscitation. If he/she is still not breathing, you must check to see if his/her heart has stopped beating.

Checking the carotid
pulse

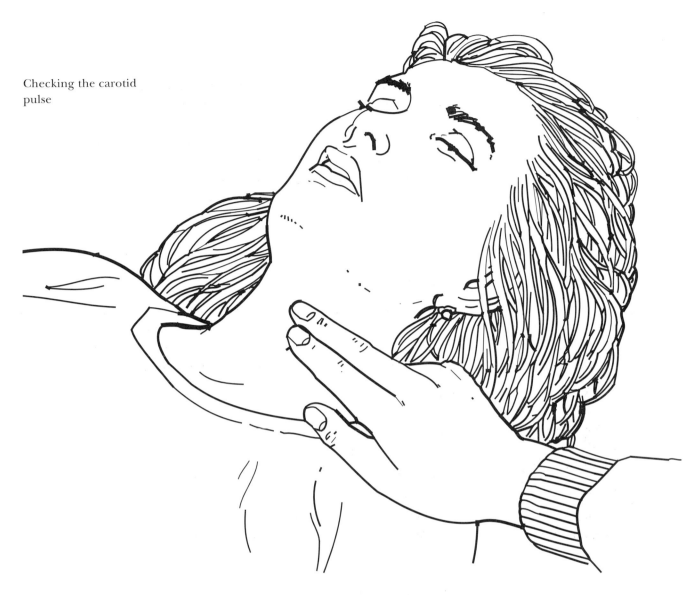

You do this by checking the **carotid** pulse in the neck. Find the pulse
by putting your fingers on the patient's Adam's Apple and then
running them up the muscle at the side of the neck. If there is no
pulse, then his/her heart has stopped beating. You must start
external chest compression very quickly.
The best way to learn how to do this is by practising with a Resusci
Anne. You could learn it from a book but, like mouth-to-mouth
resuscitation, it is better to get practical training in a class. *You must
never practise on a live person.*

When the unconscious casualty is in the recovery position and
you are waiting for the ambulance to arrive, you can keep a record
of the person's:

• pulse-rate, how fast the heart is beating

• **respiration** rate, how fast he/she is breathing

• level of consciousness.

2.1 AN, 2.3 IT **ⓒ** **Activity**

Use a computer to help you design a recording sheet so that you (or someone else) can keep track of pulse, breathing and levels of consciousness. The information should be recorded in numerical form so that it is quick and easy to do and to understand.

When it is completed, your chart could be put in a first aid kit for use in an emergency. The information it provides will be very valuable to both the ambulance staff and to the doctors and nurses in the casualty department.

Skeletal injury

Skeletons are very tough, but skeletal injuries occur when bones break and joints are dislocated. The ligaments which keep our bones in place can also be torn. It is often difficult to tell which of these things has happened without taking an X-ray.

Here are some basic rules:

- Don't move the casualty unless his/her life is in danger.
- Ask the casualty to try not to move.
- Cover any open wound with a **sterile** dressing.
- Make sure the injured part of the body cannot move. *There are special methods for this, which need to be taught by a first aid instructor.*
- Treat for shock.

Spinal injury is always very serious. It should be suspected if a person has fallen from a high place or been thrown from a horse or motorbike. A direct blow on the back by a heavy falling object could cause a similar injury. If you suspect spinal injury, *don't move the casualty or put him/her in the recovery position.* Gently turn the head to one side so that, if vomiting occurs, the casualty will not choke. If he/she is conscious, explain that it is important to stay very still.

Poisoning

Remember that poisons can be *swallowed, breathed in* or *absorbed* into the skin. If you find someone who has been poisoned, this is what you must do:

- Make sure that you aren't in danger of being affected by any poison that's still around.
- If the casualty is conscious, ask what the poison was. Don't delay doing this. He/she might become unconscious at any time.
- Call an ambulance.

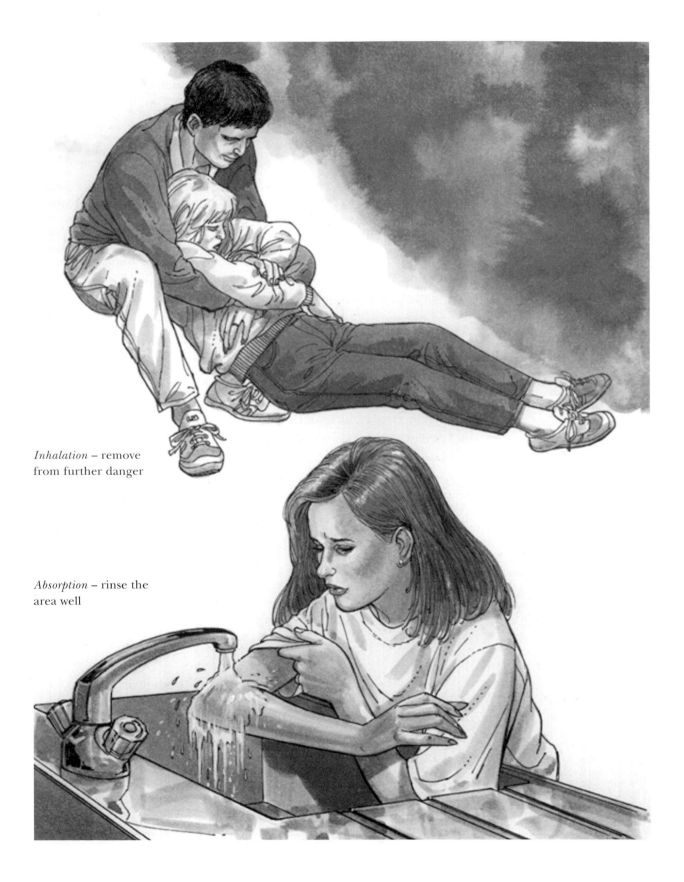

Inhalation – remove from further danger

Absorption – rinse the area well

- *Do not try to make the person sick by giving salt water or anything else.*
- If you know that the poison was corrosive (burning) or you see signs of burning around the lips, it is important to give sips of water or milk to dilute the poison. Don't encourage vomiting as this will cause more burning as the poison comes back up.
- Gently sponge away traces of poison.
- If you find the poison container, this should go to the hospital with the casualty.
- If the person is sick, put a sample into a plastic bag or a jar and send this to the hospital as well.
- Stay calm and reassure the casualty.
- If he/she becomes unconscious, put him/her into the recovery position and check the breathing regularly until help arrives. If the breathing stops, you will need to start mouth-to-mouth resuscitation.

Burns and scalds

The care procedures for all burns and scalds are the same. The whole area affected should be *cooled* as quickly as possible. Cooling the burn or scald does two things:

- It reduces pain and swelling.
- It helps to slow down fluid loss because the cold makes damaged blood vessels close.

If you burn your finger, you should hold it under the cold tap or in a cup of cold water for *ten minutes* or until the pain goes away.

A quick way to cool a larger area of skin is to soak a towel in cold water and wrap it round the burnt part. Other ways are:

- pouring water over it, or
- soaking it in a sink or bath.

Cool the burn with lots of water

If someone's clothes catch fire you must put out the flames. Without oxygen, a flame cannot burn. The person may be running around in a panic. Push the person to the ground and smother the flames with:

- a cushion
- a towel
- by lying down on top of the person.

Don't remove any fabric that is sticking to the burnt skin. Don't put on any antiseptic creams or ointments. Just cool with water.

Once the pain has eased:

- Remove anything tight, for example rings or a belt, before any swelling starts.
- Cover the area with a sterile, non-stick dressing, if you have one. If not, any clean, non-fluffy material will do, such as handkerchiefs, tea towels, torn up sheets or pillowcases.
- If body fluids leak through the dressing, *don't remove it.* Add another layer on top.
- *There is a great danger of shock.* Lie the injured person down, keep him/her warm and give sips of water until reaching hospital. You may save a life by doing this.

When chemicals are splashed on skin:
- wear disposable gloves
- hold affected area under running water for 20 minutes
- carefully remove any clothing that has chemicals on it
- dress the wound
- take the injured person to hospital.

Activity

You are sitting in the kitchen doing homework while your sister is making tea. She lifts the chip pan from the cooker, but it is so hot that she cries out and drops it with a crash on the tiled floor.

The fat spills out of the pan and splashes all over her face and bare arms before spreading across the floor.

Discuss, in pairs, what you would do next.

Here is what you should do:

- Switch off the cooker.
- Sit your sister down by the kitchen sink.
- Stay calm and tell her what you are doing at each stage.
- Soak clean tea towels in cold water and gently lay these on all the burned places.
- Encourage her to sip water.
- Call an ambulance.

Dressing wounds

When skin has been broken the wound needs to be covered. Covering it will do three things:

- control bleeding by encouraging the blood to clot
- prevent germs from entering the body through the cut
- reduce pain by covering the nerve endings which are open to the air.

Here are guidelines for the correct way to dress an open wound:

If the wound is small:

- Clean it first under running water.

If the wound is large:

- Control heavy bleeding immediately by putting a temporary dressing over the wound and pressing firmly. The casualty may be able to do this for him/herself.

Then follow this procedure:

- Wash your hands well.
- Clean the area around the wound with cotton wool balls and **cetrimide solution** (1%) or clean water. Wipe the dirt away from the wound by making overlapping strokes. Move outwards from near the wound edge. Make sure not to touch the open wound. Use fresh cotton wool for each stroke (see diagram).
- Cover the wound with a dressing which is large enough to go beyond the edges of the wound to undamaged skin. The best dressings are the pre-packed, non-stick type which are sterile until the packet is opened. In an emergency, you may not have a first aid kit and you will have to make do with a piece of clean, non-fluffy fabric. This should be covered with a thick pad and bandaged or taped in place.

Dressing wounds and bandaging are practical skills which are taught in first aid classes. You need to practise these skills.

When glass is sticking out of a wound:

- put pressure *around* the wound but *not on* it
- raise the part of the body which is wounded
- cover the wound gently with thin material (for example gauze)
- bandage *around* the wound but *not on* it
- take the injured person to the hospital.

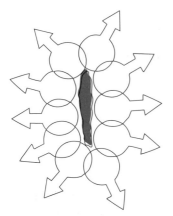

Use overlapping strokes away from the wound

2.1, 2.2 C 2.3 IT **©** **Project**

This project requires you to prepare and deliver a ten-minute presentation to your group on emergency care skills.

1 **Choose one of the following topics:**
   - asphyxia
   - shock
   - burns and scalds
   - heat exhaustion and heat stroke
   - bleeding
   - poisoning
   - heart attack
   - skeletal injuries
   - stroke
   - electric shock.

2 **Prepare your presentation making sure you include:**
   - signs and symptoms
   - care procedures
   - information about whether and how to call in the emergency services
   - your limitations in assisting at this emergency.

3 **Don't forget to do an action plan.**

4 **Think about reinforcing your information with handouts or visual aids. For example, you could wordprocess a handout listing the main points of your talk. You may wish to include a flow-chart or diagram, or to illustrate your talk with a poster or illustrations.**

   The basic facts about all these topics are in this study unit, but you could find out more by looking in first aid books and talking to first aiders or health professionals.

3

Health and safety principles

In sections 1 and 2, you learned about different types of emergencies and how to deal with them. You should be clear now about what you can and cannot do in an emergency.

In this section you will learn more about possible risks of infection and how to reduce them. You will also find out about ways of preventing accidents.

Shove over, there's room for all of us!

Preventing infection

As carers, you may be working with babies and children, or with sick or old people. Such vulnerable people must be protected from **germs**.

Germ is the name we use for the harmful **micro-organisms** which are all around us. They are so tiny that you cannot see them without a microscope. It is hard to imagine, but 80 thousand germs could fit on the head of a pin.

Micro-organisms are all around us, and all over everyone's skin. In order to survive, they need *warmth*, *moisture* and *food*. Two areas of the body which provide these conditions are armpits and noses which are warm and damp and have a supply of body fluids for the micro-organisms to feed on.

Infection occurs when harmful micro-organisms enter the body. They multiply and produce **toxins** or poisons, which give us the symptoms of illness.

Fly eggs found on food

A TAKEAWAY cafe owner has been fined £750 for selling kebabs with fly eggs on them.

Lorry driver Nigel Ross had already taken a bite when his wife Karen spotted the tiny white specks.

She contacted Erewash health officers the next day and they identified them, Ilkeston magistrates were told.

Prosecuting, Brendan Morris said there were 39 eggs of blow flies and blue bottles. Checks were carried out on Leroy's kebab shop in Tamworth Road, Long Eaton, which was found to have no insect control unit.

Dead flies were found in the front window and where meat was stored and meat was left overnight and reheated for sale next day, said Mr Morris.

Mohammed Ashraf, of Clarence Road, Derby, admitted selling contaminated kebabs. In addition to the fine he must pay £50 costs.

Miss Amerjeet Sandhu, defending, said he had been in business for ten years without a problem.

He had now installed a fly killer which was left on 24 hours a day.

Magistrate Mrs Margaret Boyd said they took account of it being his first offence.

"We could have imposed a much more severe penalty. It could have been many thousands of pounds," she warned.

Micro-organisms can get into the body in four main ways:
- through a break in the skin caused by a cut or an injection
- through a break in a mucous membrane, like the inside of the mouth, anus or vagina
- by being breathed in
- by being swallowed in food.

An illness is **infectious** when the micro-organisms can be passed easily from one person to another. When someone coughs or sneezes and another person breathes in the infected air they may become ill themselves.

An illness is said to be **contagious** when it can be spread only by touching. Infection can happen in two ways, by **direct infection** and by **indirect infection**.

Direct infection

Harmful micro-organisms can be passed on directly
- by kissing
- by sexual contact
- by touching broken skin
- by injection with a dirty needle
- by droplets of moisture.

Infection by droplets of moisture is the most common example of direct infection. Invisible droplets of moisture pass from our mouths every time we breath out or speak. Someone with a sore throat or a cold will breathe out infective micro-organisms. A sneeze or a cough can shoot the droplets over a long distance. Think for a minute what could happen if Una, the senior nursery nurse at Greenfields, were to sneeze without covering her mouth and nose during story-time.

Indirect infection

Mice, rats, cockroaches and flies all carry micro-organisms which are harmful to humans. Food which has been contaminated by any of these creatures will cause food poisoning in the people who eat it.

Think what might happen at Hillview if flies had contaminated the chicken salads for the residents' tea. You may not be surprised to discover that *hands are the main source of indirect infection.* Hands are warm and moist. They easily pick up droplet infection from the air.

2.2 AN **C** **Project**

Task 1

The area of a pin-head is about 1 square millimetre. Try to work out the area of your hand in square millimetres. It may help to think of your hand as a square with five rectangles stuck onto it.

Multiply your answer by 80 thousand to find out how many germs would fit onto your unwashed hands. Write your answer to the nearest million.

The population of Great Britain and Northern Ireland is about 57 million.

**Complete the sentence:
'There are about _____ times as many germs on my unwashed hands as there are people in the UK.'**

Task 2

Design a poster or leaflet for the kitchen or toilets in your school, college or workplace. It should encourage people to wash their hands.

Preventing infection at an emergency

It is important to remember that germs can be passed both ways:
- from you to the casualty
- from the casualty to you.

Two very serious illnesses which you need to be aware of are **AIDS** and **hepatitis B**. AIDS is short for:
- Acquired – from the blood or body fluids of an infected person
- Immune – your body's defence system against infection
- Deficiency – not working well enough
- Syndrome – a group of symptoms.

AIDS is caused by the Human Immuno-deficiency Virus (**HIV**). An infected person carries this **virus** in body fluids.

HIV/AIDS is not *contagious,* so it cannot be transferred from one person to another by breathing in droplets from the air or by touching an object that the infected person has touched, for example a cup or a loo seat.

HIV/AIDS is very *infectious* in circumstances where the body fluids of one person pass into the body fluids of another. The commonest way for this to happen is during sexual contact.

When a woman is **HIV positive** (is infected with HIV), there is a possibility that her children will be born with it.

Hepatitis B is an illness which is also transferred through infected blood or semen passing from one person to another. However, it can also be transferred through saliva.

A **vaccine** is available which will protect you from hepatitis B. It is expensive and not available free to everyone. If you are a regular first aider or work in a health or social care setting, you should ask about having a **vaccination.**

During a health emergency, you need to be aware of the risks that these illnesses pose to yourself and to the casualty.

It is possible to become infected with hepatitis B by giving mouth-to-mouth resuscitation. However, no cases have been recorded so far. The main way that **cross-infection** can take place is through passing blood from an infected person into the open wound of an uninfected person.

Here are some guidelines for protecting yourself and the casualty in a health emergency:

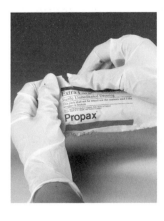

- Make sure all cuts and grazes on your own hands are covered with waterproof dressings.
- Wear disposable gloves if you are dealing with blood or other body fluids. If you haven't got gloves, you could use plastic sandwich bags.
- If you have no gloves or bags, make sure you wash your hands well after you have been in contact with blood or body fluids.
- When you are sure that the injured person is comfortable and not in danger, mop up any spilt blood and body fluids. If you have any bleach, a solution of 1 part bleach to 10 parts water is recommended for this.
- All soiled dressings, including the gloves and mopping-up cloth, should be tied up in a plastic bag. You can either burn this or take it to your local Health Centre and ask them to get rid of it.

Safe lifting techniques

The best advice about moving an injured person is *don't do it unless it's absolutely essential.* The main dangers involved in ignoring this advice are:

• you may injure the casualty even more
• you may injure yourself.

Lifting without injuring yourself

As with mouth-to-mouth resuscitation and heart massage, correct lifting is a skill that must be practised. Many employers offer training courses in lifting techniques. This is because there are strict Health and Safety laws that protect workers and those in their care. If you have to move someone in an emergency, remember to:

• Get close to the casualty.
• Place your feet slightly apart with one foot in front of the other.
• Bend at your knees, not at your hips.
• Keep your back straight and upright.
• Make sure you have a firm grip.
• Lift straight up as close to your body as possible.

Remember that you should move an injured person only if he/she is at risk of further injury or needs to be moved to a safer place. *Move someone who is seriously injured only if their life is in immediate danger.*

Right and wrong approaches to lifting

Wrong

Right

Special lifting techniques

The method you use to move an injured person will depend on whether:

- other people are available to help
- the injured person is conscious
- the injured person can walk
- how the casualty is injured.

Drag method

Cradle method

Human crutch

Pick-a-back

The fore-and-aft carry

The two-handed seat

Whenever you try to move a casualty, remember to explain what you are doing and give plenty of reassurance.

The following notes briefly describe some safe methods for moving a casualty. *It is important to get proper instruction and supervised practice before using these methods.*

If only one person is available

The most difficult problem is to move an unconscious casualty when there is no help available. This can be done by putting your arms under the casualty's armpits and *dragging* from behind. The same method could be used to move a large person who is conscious but can't walk. Remember to bend at the knees and have your feet close to the casualty.

If a child or a lighter person needs moving, you may be able to *cradle* him/her in your arms. Remember to bend at the knees and get close before lifting.

You should try to give someone a '*pick-a-back*' only if he/she is conscious and is light enough to lift. He/she must be able to put their arms round your neck and hold on. Again, you must bend at the knees and stand as close as possible in front of the casualty before lifting.

Someone who is conscious and able to walk can be supported more easily using the '*human crutch*' method. Stand close to the casualty's weaker side and put his/her arm round your shoulder. Put your arm around his/her waist and hold on to the clothing. Take small steps and move together.

If two people are available

With two people, the dragging method can be turned into a lift. The second person can lift the casualty's legs by supporting them from underneath, just above the knees. Both lifters must remember to get close in to the casualty and bend at the knees.

Two helpers can also lift a casualty in the following way:

- Stand facing each other, either side of the injured person.
- Stand very close and bend at the knees.
- Reach behind the casualty's back and cross arms.
- Get a good grip on the casualty's clothing. The waistband is best.
- Pass your other hand under the casualty's knees and hold on to each other's wrists.
- Hold on tight and stand up. Remember to keep your back straight and use your leg muscles to take the weight.

Activity

For each of the health emergencies described below, decide:

- whether or not you would move the injured person
- which method of lifting you would use and why.

1   You are on the evening shift at Hillview. When you take Mr Stringer's bedtime cocoa, you discover that he has fallen out of bed again. He assures you that he is not in any pain at all, but he just can't manage to get up.

2   You are enjoying an afternoon in the park with your three-year-old nieces Julie and Suzie. They are chasing each other around the pond when Julie trips and falls. You hear her roar from a hundred yards away. As you approach, you see that both her knees are badly grazed.

3   You are jogging with a friend along the canal bank one spring evening. As you approach a boarded-up warehouse, you hear a cry and decide to investigate. You follow the sound of whimpering. In the dim light, you see a young man lying in a heap of rubble. A large girder is pinning him to the ground.

Here are our suggestions.

1 You should not try to move Mr Stringer on your own. Ask another carer to help you and use a two-person lift.

2 Julie is conscious and very sore but not badly injured. You could cradle her in your arms and take her to the first aid post. Don't forget to comfort Suzie as well.

3 This is a difficult decision. If the girder has fallen, it is likely that other parts of the building could also collapse. You will have to use your judgement. You may be able to lift the girder together (remembering to use correct lifting techniques), then use a two-person lift to get the casualty out of the building. If it is too heavy, one person should go to call the emergency services while the other person stays with the casualty.

Preventing accidents and emergencies

Most people who work in health and care settings will need training in safe lifting. All employers are responsible for providing training of this kind. Your employer must make sure that:

- the place you work in, the equipment you use and the ways of using it are safe and do not put your health at risk
- you are given any information and training that you need and that you are properly supervised
- all equipment and chemicals are stored safely
- your workplace is pleasant to work in, not too crowded, warm, well lit and well ventilated.

Activity

Read the following descriptions of accidents. Make notes on what could have been done to prevent them.

Accident 1
Mrs Davis fell badly in the reception area at Hillview just after the floor had been washed.

Accident 2
Brian brushed against the broken corner of the kitchen table at Hillview and his leg was cut.

Accident 3
Milly fell off the swing at Greenfields Day Nursery and grazed her knees.

Accident 4
Una twisted her ankle when she stepped on an empty plastic bottle that had been left on the stairs.

Accident 5
Mr Simpkins got a nasty electric shock when he switched the hand drier on in the men's toilets.

Employers are not the only people who have a responsibility to guard against accidents. Employees are expected to be careful and to help to make their workplace safe.

1 The person who mopped the reception floor at Hillview should have put up a sign warning people about the danger of slipping.

2 The kitchen table may have been damaged for some time. Had someone reported it?

An employer is responsible for making sure that workers know about safe practice. If the employees knew they had to do these things, they might get into trouble for not doing them.

3/4 It is difficult to say whether the accidents to Una and to Milly could have been avoided. Was there enough supervision in the playground? Where had the bottle on the stairs come from? Had someone failed to clear it away after a play session?

5 Mr Simpkins's electric shock might have been the result of faulty equipment. All electrical equipment in a workplace has to be checked for safety at least once a year. Had the hand drier been checked recently?

If an employer or employee has caused a serious accident, then he/she could be taken to court. Prevention of accidents is something we must all take seriously.

Electrical safety

Accidents involving electricity are often avoidable. Common causes of such accidents are:
- faulty electrical equipment
- frayed electric cables
- faulty switches
- long, trailing cables
- overloaded power points
- misuse of electrical equipment.

Most of these can be avoided. Employers and workers can agree about what to do. One person should take responsibility as 'safety representative' in the workplace.

Fire precautions

There are several common causes of fires in health and care settings. These include:
- careless use of **flammable** substances, including cleaning materials and pressurised containers
- careless smoking, especially when matches and cigarette ends are thrown away
- electrical problems.

Staff at places like Hillview and Greenfields have to safeguard against the risk of fire. They must also know what to do when a fire is discovered. These precautions might include:

• a good fire alarm system which may include smoke alarms and sprinklers

• ways of preventing the spread of fire, for example self-closing fire doors

• fire extinguishers that are checked regularly

• other fire-fighting equipment, like fire blankets

• safe ways to leave the building during a fire

• clear instructions displayed in every room about what to do in case of fire.

Find out why we need different types of fire extinguishers

What to do if you discover a fire

• Push the fire alarm button.

• Get everyone out of the building as quickly as possible.

• Call the fire brigade by ringing 999.

• If you have time, close all doors and windows to stop the spread of the fire.

Practise fire drills to make sure people learn what to do and where to go if there is a fire.

2.2, 2.3 C, 2.3 IT **C** **Project**

The aim of this project is to prepare a report covering the health and safety principles you have studied in this section.

1 **Invent a health or social care setting like Greenfields Day Nursery or Hillview Rest Home. Imagine that you are a visiting inspector finding out whether this is a safe establishment both for staff and clients.**

2 **Write a report of your findings which should include the following:**
   - what staff are expected to do to prevent contamination
   - what staff are taught about dressing wounds hygienically
   - how staff are trained to lift
   - what the rules are about electrical safety
   - what is done to prevent fire and what happens if there is one
   - what is done to prevent injury, for example falling on slippery surfaces.

3 **Before you begin, write your action plan. Think about what information you will need to do this task and how you will find it. Set yourself a time for collecting information and a time for writing your project.**

   There is some basic information in this booklet, but, if you are aiming for a *merit* or *distinction*, you will need to look at other sources of evidence, for example:
   - you could find out what the law says
   - you could find out what health and safety policies other establishments have.

   You might try the following places for more information:
   - library
   - health information service
   - trade union health and safety officers
   - nursing homes
   - day nurseries
   - community centres.

Summary

In this study unit you have learned about health emergencies – what they are, how they may happen, and how to deal with them. You have covered many of the most common and most serious health emergencies so that you can identify and distinguish between them and take emergency action.

Even though you may not be fully trained in first aid, you can still offer valuable help and you may even save a life by recognising the urgency of a situation and knowing how to contact the emergency services.

You now know how important it is to look after yourself in emergency situations and to protect the casualty from further harm while providing assistance before the professionals arrive. A good first aid kit, safe lifting techniques and a knowledge of health and safety procedures will help you to help others with confidence.

Finally, you have looked at health and safety principles, including preventing the spread of infection through the use of good hygiene. You have seen that health and safety requirements, especially in public places, should be clear to everyone. You now have the basic skills and knowledge to help anyone in an emergency.

If you want to learn more practical first aid skills, you should contact your local college, library or the St John's Ambulance service who should be able to tell you about first aid courses in your area.

Review activity

You have now completed your work on this study unit. Spend some time reviewing what you have achieved.

1 Grading themes

For Intermediate GNVQs you can achieve a higher grading depending on how much initiative and independent action you take in the areas of:

- planning
- information-gathering.

Action planning

Look over all the projects you worked on for this unit:
- Did you complete detailed Action Plans for each project?
- How much support did you need from your teacher/tutor to complete the plans?
- Did you regularly review and update your plans?
- How successful were you in achieving your plans and targets?
- Were there any areas where you didn't achieve your aims? Why was this?
- What would you have done differently?

Information-gathering

Look over all the projects you worked on for this unit:
- Did you successfully identify the sorts of information you needed to complete projects and activities?
- Did you successfully gather the information you needed? How did you do this?
- How would you assess the quality of information you gathered? Was it:
– useful and relevant?
– appropriate for your needs?
– accurate and complete?

- Were there any areas where you were not able to gather the information you needed? Why was this?
- What would you have done differently?

2 Performance criteria and range

Look at the standards for this GNVQ unit. Work through the PCs for the unit and check that you have done work that will help you meet each one. Do this by noting down the PC number against the relevant work.

Finally, check through the information given under the range.
- Do you understand everything that is listed in the range?
- Are you confident that the work you have done on projects covers the range properly?

3 Core skills

If you have completed the projects in this study unit, you should have covered the core skills listed below. You may find that you have also covered other core skills: look through the standards and decide whether there are any others which you could include in your evidence for this unit.

Communication Elements 2.1, 2.2, 2.3, 2.4.
Application of Number Element 2.2
Information Technology Element 2.3.

Answers to activities

page 113   The correct order of the instructions is: (f), (d), (c), (a), (e), (g), (b)

page 118   disposable plastic gloves
a box of adhesive plasters (various sizes)
packaged sterile dressings (various sizes)
adhesive tape for dressings
large triangular bandages
rolls of crepe bandage
cotton wool for cleaning (not dressing) wounds
tweezers
scissors
safety pins
small notepad and
pencil

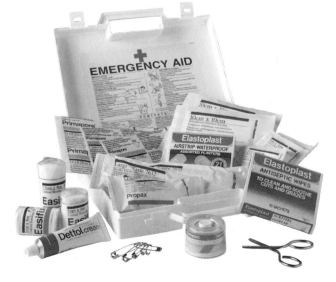

Glossary

ABC The vital needs of an unconscious casualty which must be maintained: open Airway, adequate Breathing, sufficient Circulation

Adam's Apple hard lump at the front of your neck, more prominent in men

AIDS Aquired Immune Deficiency Syndrome. People who are infected with HIV will almost always develop AIDS.

airway the route from outside the body into the lungs, normally through the windpipe

angina condition which results from insufficient blood flowing to the heart through the coronary arteries; often the result of excitement or exertion

arteries large tubes that carry blood from the heart to the rest of the body

artificial respiration helping a casualty to breathe by blowing into the lungs

asphyxia potentially fatal condition caused by insufficient oxygen reaching the tissues of the body. *See also* **suffocation**

asthma condition in which the muscles of the airway tighten and go into spasms causing breathing difficulties

body fluids blood, plasma that leaks from burns or blisters, saliva, urine

bruise injury caused by a blow resulting in bleeding under the skin without breaking it; the skin becomes discoloured

capillaries tiny tubes that branch off from arteries carrying blood to every part of your body

cardiac arrest the heart stops beating completely; commonly known as a heart attack

cardiac massage rhythmic pressing of the chest to compress the heart and stimulate it to pump blood through the arteries; used only when the heart has stopped beating

carotid arteries the arteries in the neck that are used to check someone's pulse

casualty an injured person

caustic chemical or liquid which can burn or eat away your skin, for example, acid

cetrimide solution a mild antiseptic

compound fracture one in which the broken bone pokes through a wound

conscious awake

contagious describes a disease which is spread by touching

cross-infection when infection is passed from you to the casualty or from the casualty to you.

digestion the process of breaking down food so that it can be used by the body to produce energy

direct infection infection caused by micro-organisms being passed directly from an infected person to another

dislocation when bones go 'out of joint'; shoulders, elbows,

knees are often dislocated

epileptic attacks fits causing unconsciousness, and muscle spasms caused by an electrical disorder in the brain

external chest compression *see* **cardiac massage**

first aid the help that you can give a casualty before the emergency services arrive

flammable catches fire very easily

fracture a broken or cracked bone

germ harmful micro-organism which can grow and develop

haemorrhaging bleeding

health emergency a situation in which someone needs first aid

heart attack this happens when a blood clot blocks a coronary artery, preventing blood from reaching the heart

heat exhaustion a condition caused by loss of water and salt, usually through sweating in very hot conditions – can lead to headaches, dizziness and vomiting

hepatitis B infectious disease of the liver that may be fatal

HIV positive the term used to describe blood which contains the Human Immuno-deficiency Virus, that causes AIDS

hypoglycaemia a condition in which low blood sugar may result in dizziness or loss of consciousness, often in people with diabetes

indirect infection infection caused by micro-organisms passed on through food or on dirty surfaces rather than directly from one person to another

infectious disease which can be passed on from one person to another, for example chickenpox. A heart attack is not infectious

inhalation breathing in

ligaments strong fibres that hold bones together at joints

micro-organisms tiny living things, often bacteria which may cause disease

mouth-to-mouth resuscitation breathing into an unconscious casualty's mouth in order to supply oxygen and hopefully to stimulate independent breathing

mucous membrane slimy, wet surfaces lining the parts of our bodies which communicate with the outside world, for example the inside of the nose or mouth

paralysed unable to move or feel

pulse beating or throbbing of arteries which can be felt as blood is pumped through them

recovery position a special way of resting an unconscious person on his/her side so that the airway is clear

reflexes automatic movements of the body, for example twitches, coughing

respiration breathing

resuscitation bringing back to life or consciousness

shock condition of weakness caused when not enough oxygen-carrying blood is passing round the body; it may be fatal

skeletal injury damage to the skeleton or bones, i.e. fractures, dislocations or sprains

sprain injured ligaments around a joint causing pain and swelling

sterile free from germs

stroke condition in which the blood supply to part of the brain is cut off by a blood clot or a ruptured artery

suffocation occurs when air cannot get to the lungs, usually caused by an obstruction of the windpipe. *See also* **asphyxia**

toxin poisonous substance produced in the body

unconscious unable to respond normally

vaccination attempt to provide immunity to certain diseases by introducing a small amount of the disease substance, for example smallpox, into the body by injection or swallowing

vaccine a substance that helps to build the body's defences against an infectious disease

vein large tubes that carry blood from the rest of the body back to the heart

virus infectious micro-organism causing illness and disease

vomit substance that is ejected from the stomach when someone is sick

Health
and social care
services

Contents

Introduction

Most of us take it for granted that when we are ill we can see a doctor and that our parents don't have to pay for us to go to school. This is because there is a *welfare state* in the UK which provides free medical services and education. But many older people who were children in the 1930s and 1940s can remember a time when the situation was very different. The following extract is taken from a description of children who were evacuated from London and other major cities to the country during World War II.

Except for a small number the children were filthy, and in this district we have never seen so many verminous children lacking any knowledge of clean and hygienic habits. Furthermore, it appears they were unbathed for months. One child was suffering from scabies and the majority had it in their hair and the others had dirty septic sores all over their bodies.

Their clothing was in a deplorable condition, some of the children being literally sewn into their ragged little garments ... condition of their boots and shoes – there was hardly a child with a whole pair and most of the children were walking on the ground – no soles, and just uppers hanging together...

It seems incredible that such poverty was so widespread in Britain only 50 years ago. In a study of poverty in York in 1936, it was estimated that almost half the children of working-class parents spent at least the first five years of their lives suffering from poverty and malnutrition.

Everything was transformed between 1945 and 1950, when the Government set up the welfare state through a series of Acts of Parliament. The aim of the new legislation was revolutionary: to give everyone the right to free healthcare, free education and help with money and housing if needed. Nowadays, the Welfare State has developed into an extensive system of health and social care services, providing healthcare, education, housing and national insurance against illness, unemployment and old age.

'Town Children Through Country Eyes, 1940', National Federation of Women's Institutes, in *Britain Since 1800: Towards the Welfare State.* H. Martin

1 Providing health and social care services

In the welfare state, services can be divided into two main types:

- Health services are concerned with looking after people's health. Examples of people who work in the health services are doctors, nurses and dentists.
- Social care services are concerned with looking after people who are not able to look after themselves very well. Social services include services for children, young people, elderly people and people with disabilities. Examples of people who work in the social services include social workers, **probation officers**, home care assistants and residential care workers.

Find out what you know already about these services by doing the next activity.

Many different people are involved in providing health and social care services in the welfare state. Without their skill and dedication, there would be no welfare state. These are just some of the jobs people do:

Can you think of any others?
Write a list of as many as you can think of.

Everyone's list will be different but you might have included:

- hospital doctor
- physiotherapist
- social worker

- speech therapist
- psychiatric nurse
- residential care assistant.

In the rest of this study unit, we will be looking in detail at how the health and social care services are organised, who uses them and who provides them. We will also see how people can gain access to these services. Finally we will consider people's rights, for example the rights to education and freedom from discrimination, and how health and social care services can uphold these rights.

Activity

In a group or on your own, look at the following list of services and divide them into two types: *health services* and *social services*. On a separate piece of paper, list the services under the two headings shown below. The first one has been done for you.

- baby clinic
- GP
- chiropody
- nursery
- meals on wheels
- day centre for people with disabilities
- residential home for old people
- social services transport
- hospital physiotherapy
- optician.

Health service	Social service
baby clinic	

You may be able to think of other health and social services. If so, add these to your list. Check your answers on page 190.

Organisation of health and social services

Health and social services are organised in different ways in different countries. In the next section we will be looking briefly at the way in which they are organised in England, Wales and Northern Ireland.

Organisation of health services

Healthcare is mainly provided by the National Health Service (NHS). A government department, the Department of Health (DoH), has overall responsibility for the NHS. It is responsible for the NHS Executive (NHSE) which is the head office of the NHS.

The NHSE is in charge of running the service and directs the activities of the regional health authorities (RHAs).

In the NHS there is a system of *purchasing and providing*. Under this system an RHA has a block of money to spend on health services for the people in that region. It allocates money to:

- the family health service authority (FHSA) to pay for primary care
- the district health authority (DHA) to pay for secondary care.

The FHSAs and the DHAs then buy or **purchase** the services they need. These are supplied or **provided** by organisations from both within and outside the NHS. Providers include:

- trust hospitals
- private hospitals
- GPs.

Some GP practices (fund-holding) are also purchasers because they manage their own budgets rather than having them managed for them by an FHSA.

The RHAs are in charge of providing healthcare to people living in that region and are in turn responsible for the FHSAs and the DHAs in the region.

FHSAs are responsible for **primary healthcare** (GPs, dentists, district nurses, etc.) and DHAs are responsible for **secondary healthcare** (mainly hospitals) in the district.

There are also **trusts** which are directly responsible to the NHSE rather than to the RHAs. Trusts are independent organisations which have contracts to run certain healthcare services.

Organisation of social services

In both England and Wales local authorities are responsible for providing social services, usually through social services offices. The DoH advises on best practice through its Social Services Inspectorate but is not involved in the day-to-day running of social services. Local authorities are called County Councils, Metropolitan Districts or London Boroughs, depending on where you live.

2.3C 🄖 **Activity**

In Northern Ireland health and social services are managed together by four health and social service boards.

Read the information on the organisation of health services again. Look at the chart below. Fill in the empty boxes to show the way the NHS is organised. Two boxes have already been done for you.

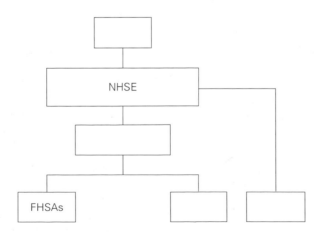

The organisation with overall control is the DoH so you should have put that in the top box. Under the DoH is the NHSE with responsibility for running the service. It directs the activities of the RHAs. Under the RHAs are the FHSAs (primary healthcare) and the DHAs (secondary healthcare). The trusts report directly to the NHSE.

Read the information on the organisation of health services again if you are not quite clear about the structure.

Did you know?

- The total population of the UK is about 57 million. It is estimated that 97 per cent of people in the UK are registered with a GP.

- Total **gross expenditure** on the NHS in 1992–93 was £35.8 billion compared with £11.4 billion in 1981–82.

- Total spending on family health services in 1990 was £4,669.3 million, divided as follows:

Medical	£1,585.8 million
Pharmaceutical	£2,325.8 million
Dental	£586.6 million
Ophthalmological	£98.3 million

2.3 AN **⊙** **Activity**

Read the *Did you know?* information carefully and answer the following questions on healthcare:

1 **What was the percentage increase in expenditure on the NHS between 1981–82 and 1992–93 (not accounting for inflation)?**

2 **How many people in the UK are estimated to be registered with a GP?**

3 **Calculate the percentage spent on the different services within the family health services (medical, pharmaceutical, dental and ophthalmological). Draw a pie chart showing how the money was divided.**

Charities and voluntary organisations

So far we have looked at just the services that are provided by the State or **local authorities**. Health and social services are also provided by **voluntary organisations** and **charities.** These are organisations which are funded by gifts, donations and grants from individuals and central and local government. They do not make a profit from the help they provide.

Activity

In a group or on your own write a list on the left-hand side of a piece of paper of as many charities as you can think of. Think about any charities you have heard about on the radio or television or any sponsored charity events you have been involved in. On the right-hand side write examples of the health and/or social services provided by each of the charities you have listed.

Could you think of many charities?

We came up with the following list:

Charity	Examples of services offered
Guide Dogs for the Blind Association	Guide dogs and training for people who are blind
Women's Royal Voluntary Service (WRVS)	Meals on wheels
Childline	Freephone line for children in difficulties
British Association of Cancer United Patients and their families and friends (BACUP)	Advice, information and support for people with cancer and their families and friends
Carers' National Association	Advice, information and support for carers
National AIDS Helpline	Free and confidential advice and information about HIV and AIDS

If you want to find out more, there is a list of charities in a book called *Charities Digest* which should be in the reference section of your local library.

Private health and care services

It is also possible to get private help. Some local authorities pay for people to have private help or people who can afford it can pay for themselves. For example, some people pay to go to private hospitals or pay for private help at home. Look in the *Yellow Pages* under 'Employment Agencies and Consultants' or 'Nurses and Nursing' and you will see lists of local agencies which can provide private nursing or help at home. People also advertise for private help in magazines like *The Lady* and in national and local newspapers. Many people rely on the help of friends, family and neighbours to help them if they are ill or disabled in any way.

Advertisements from
The Lady

Complicated care

Some people need a wide range of help from health and social services. For example, an elderly person might need to go to hospital once a month, be visited at home twice a week by a **district nurse**, have a home help from social services three times a week and WRVS meals on wheels delivered every day. If someone needs several different types of help, it is important to co-ordinate the services so that everyone knows who is responsible for what. This is sometimes done by drawing up a **care plan**, which describes what help is to be provided and by whom. In the next activity you will start by looking at a care plan and identifying what services are to be provided and who is to provide them.

2.3 AN, 2.4 C Ⓒ **Activity**

Read the following case study and then answer the questions.

George Robinson is a 79-year-old widower. He is about to leave hospital after a **coronary bypass operation**. He lives alone but he has two sons who call in on him in the evenings and at weekends. He is very keen to continue to live at home when he comes out of hospital and doesn't want to go into a residential home. He is mentally alert but has difficulty in getting about and is not strong enough to do his own housework and cooking. He gets lonely during the day if he doesn't have any visitors.

Because George has a number of different needs, June, a social worker from the local authority's social services office has been appointed as his **care manager** to make sure that the help he is given is co-ordinated properly. June has already visited George in hospital to find out what help he needs in order to be able to continue living at home. After talking to the hospital staff and other people who will be involved in looking after George, June has written a care plan for him. She gives George a copy and sends copies to all the different providers of services. It would include information such as personal details and dates for further assessment as well as the following description of action required to meet George's needs.

Care plan for George Robinson

1 Hospital to inform Mr Robinson's GP (Dr Nuttall) that he is leaving hospital.

2 A **home care assistant** from social services to visit Monday, Wednesday and Friday to help with housework and shopping.

3 Wheelchair to be arranged by hospital **occupational therapist**.

4 Hand rails to be fitted in bathroom and at front door by social services. Social services also to provide a personal alarm.

5 Mr Robinson to go to Age Concern day centre once a week for the day including lunch. Transport to be provided by social services.

6 WRVS to provide meals on wheels on other days.

7 Nurse from GP surgery to visit daily for first two weeks to check on Mr Robinson's wound.

8 Hospital appointment in two weeks' time – transport to be provided by hospital.

9 Volunteer from local sixth-form college to visit Mr Robinson twice a week after college.

June Smithwick, April 1994

1 **Using the information in the care plan, make a list on a separate piece of paper of all the different services which are to be provided for George when he leaves hospital and who is to be responsible for them. Write down the following categories at the top of your paper and then decide which category each service falls under:**

Social services   Charity/voluntary   Community health   Hospital

2 **If you can, role-play with a partner the conversation between George and June after George has read the care plan. One of you should pretend to be George and the other should be June. You might be able to make a video of yourselves. Think of the kinds of things that George might want to know more about. For example:**

- When can I go home?
- Will I have any choice about which home care assistant I have?
- How long will I be able to keep the wheelchair?
- Will I have to pay for it?
- Do I have any choice about the meals provided by the WRVS?

As June, you may have to provide not only the information George needs but also some reassurance. At the end of the role-play, you should both write a short note summarising the points you have covered and what has been agreed.
You can then swap roles if you have time.

3 Find out what a personal alarm is and what it looks like. Draw a two-dimensional illustration of a personal alarm.

Co-ordinating care

As you can see from your answer to the first part of the activity, co-ordinating the range of services needed by someone like George can be quite complicated. In George's case, a care manager has been appointed to make sure that everyone knows what has been agreed and to ensure that everyone does what he/she has agreed to do. If the care needed is complex, it can help to draw a chart to show all the different services similar to the following:

Social services	Charity/voluntary	Community health	Hospital
transport to day centre	meals on wheels	home visits from nurse	inform GP
home care assistant	day centre		provide wheelchair
hand rails	sixth former		out-patient appointment and transport
personal alarm			

People with disabilities sometimes need a range of health and social services too. In the next activity you will be looking at the services provided for Meera, an 18-year-old woman who has **cerebral palsy**. Her mind is not affected by her condition but she is unable to walk, is blind and has difficulties speaking. She lives at home with her father, Jay.

2.3C, 2.3 IT **C** **Activity**

Read the following account of Meera's week.

Monday

Meera goes to a social education centre run by the local authority. In the morning, she learns how to use a photocopier and in the afternoon the students go swimming. She is taken to the centre and brought home in a minibus provided by social services. In the evening Jay has to go out to a meeting but Meera's aunt comes to the house to help Meera get ready for bed and stay with her until Jay gets home.

Tuesday

Meera has a hospital appointment in the morning. Jay takes her in the car. In the afternoon a physiotherapist from the local surgery visits Meera at home and spends an hour with her doing exercises to prevent her joints from stiffening.

Wednesday

Meera spends the day at a centre run by the Royal National Institute for the Blind. She is learning to use a computer and hopes to work as a computer programmer eventually.

Thursday

Jay works on Thursdays. A home care assistant from social services comes in the morning to prepare Meera's lunch. In the afternoon a volunteer from a charity called Crossroads Care takes Meera out for a drive and stays with her until Jay comes home.

Friday

In the morning, an occupational therapist from social services visits Meera and Jay to measure up for a new wheelchair. In the afternoon, they prepare for the following day when Meera is going to a holiday centre for people with disabilities run by a charity called John Groom's Association for the Disabled. Jay is having a holiday too to give him a break from caring.

Using a computer, draw a chart like the one for George on page 157 showing the different services which have been provided for Meera and Jay. Use these headings again:

Social services	Charity/voluntary	Community health	Hospital

Your chart should have included the following services under each heading:

Social services: Social education centre and transport, home care assistant, wheelchair (occupational therapist)

Charity/voluntary: RNIB centre, Crossroads Care attendant, holiday centre

Community health: Physiotherapist

Hospital: Out-patient appointment

As you can see, Meera and Jay get quite a lot of help from social services and voluntary organisations. But if Meera did not have her father and her aunt to look after her at home, she would need a lot more help and might have to move into a residential care home.

People with disabilities

- There are more than 6.2 million adults with disabilities in the UK.

- People with disabilities represent 14.2 per cent of the total adult population.

- People with disabilities make up only 1 per cent of the workforce.

- 31 per cent of people with disabilities have jobs, compared with 69 per cent of the general population of working age.

Health and social services in your area

Although health authorities and local authorities are required by law to provide a certain range of health and social services, the way in which these services are organised and provided varies across the country. In the rest of this section you will be working on a project to find out what services are available where you live and how they are organised.

2.2 AN, 2.2 IT **C** **Project**

This project is about finding out about local services. It will involve:

- planning how you are going to find out what services are available in your area

- doing the research

- designing and producing an information leaflet for people living in your area describing those services.

If you are not sure about how to plan your project, look again at the induction booklet for Intermediate level.

To complete this project you will probably need to follow these steps:

1 **Find out which health authority and which local authority you live in and what area they cover (they may not cover exactly the same area). Find out how many people live in the health authority and how many live in the local authority. You should be able to get this information from:**

- the town hall or civic centre

- the library

- a Citizens' Advice Bureau (CAB) – in the phone book under 'Citizens''

- the community health council – in the phone book under 'Community'.

If you live in Northern Ireland you will need to find out which health and social service board area you live in.

2 **Find out what health and social services are available in your area including those provided by voluntary organisations and private companies and where they are located. For each of the following,**

find out how many of them there are, who provides them and where they are located:

- hospitals
- GP surgeries/health centres
- dentists
- opticians
- chiropodists
- baby clinics

- day centres for elderly people
- day centres for people with disabilities
- residential and nursing homes for elderly people
- residential homes for people with disabilities
- residential homes for children
- nurseries for young children.

To get this information you will need to contact a number of organisations – either by going to see them, by telephoning or by writing.

Some of the organisations which are most likely to be able to help you include:

- the town hall or civic centre
- the DHA and FSHA – in the *Yellow Pages* under 'Health authorities and services'
- the local social services office – in the *Yellow Pages* under 'Local government'
- the DoH – telephone 071 210 4850
- a CAB
- a community health council
- a post office
- a library
- a GP's surgery
- a dentist surgery
- a hospital
- a volunteer centre or bureau – in the *Yellow Pages* under 'Volunteer' or 'Voluntary'
- private nursing agencies – in the *Yellow Pages* under 'Employment Agencies and Consultants' or 'Nurses and Nursing'
- residential care and nursing homes – in the *Yellow Pages* under 'Residential and Retirement' or 'Nursing homes'.

You may be able to think of others.

If you find examples of other services while you are doing your research, make a note of these too.

3 **Calculate how many people there are for each type of service, using your information about the size of the local population. For example, if 150,000 people live in your health authority and there are five hospitals, the ratio of people per hospital is 150,000 ÷ 5 = 30,000 to 1.**

Write your answer under the following headings:

Type of facility	Population ratio
Hospitals	30,000 per hospital

4 **Using a computer, write, design and produce an information leaflet for the people who live in your area describing the health and social services which are available and who provides them. Your leaflet should include:**

- information about who provides the services
- a map showing where the services are located
- information about how many people there are for each service.

You can either draw your own map on the computer or photocopy a map and mark on it where the different facilities are. You might be able to get a copy of a map free of charge from a local estate agent.

Your project will form part of the evidence in your portfolio.

Using health and social services

We all have a wide range of different needs in order to be able to live our daily lives.

Needs

These are definitions of 'need' from the *Longman Dictionary of the English Language*:

- 'a lack of something necessary, desirable or useful'
- 'a physiological or psychological requirement for the well-being of an organism'
- 'a condition requiring supply or relief'.

We all have a range of needs from basic ones like food and shelter to those which are more complex such as love and affection.

There are five main types of needs – these are listed below with an example for each one:

- Physical needs – to do with our bodies and our health,
  e.g. I need to eat well and keep fit.

- Social needs – to do with how we live with other people,
  e.g. I need to see my friends regularly.

- Emotional needs – to do with how we feel,
  e.g. I need someone to talk to about my problems.

- Cultural needs – to do with our background and culture,
  e.g. I need to listen to music.

- Educational needs – to do with how we learn and our intellect
  e.g. I need to learn to read and write.

Activity

Look at these pictures.

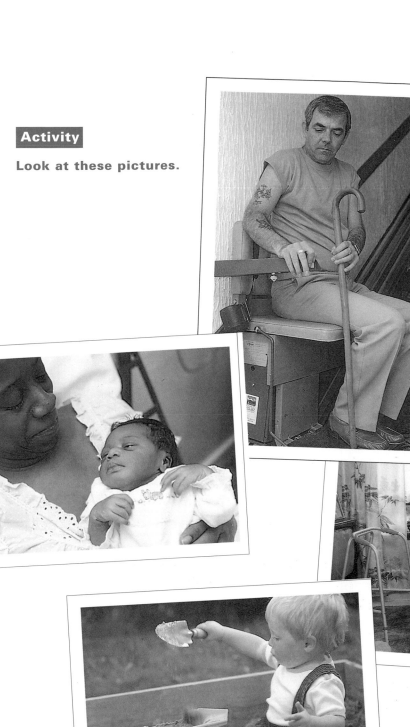

165

In a group or on your own, think about what the people in the pictures might need, using the categories from the list on p. 164: physical, social, emotional, cultural, educational. Copy the following chart onto a computer or large piece of paper. For each person, type or write at least two needs in the column marked 'Need' under the appropriate category. You will complete the 'Service' column in the next activity.

	Physical		Social		Emotional		Cultural		Educational	
	Need	Service	Need	Service	Need	Service	Need	Service	Need	Service
Elderly woman										
Man in wheelchair										
16-year-old										
New mother										
Toddler										

If you find this activity difficult, try to imagine what kinds of things you would need if you were the person. It's not always easy to imagine what it's like to be another person but this is something that people who work in the health and social services have to do all the time.

There is no 'right' answer to this activity as we are only guessing. Here are some of the possibilities:

Elderly woman

Physical needs: difficulties doing shopping and cooking, bunions on feet
Social needs: gets lonely without company
Educational: wants to learn French

Man in wheelchair

Physical needs: home not suitable for wheelchair, muscle weakness, transport problems
Educational needs: can no longer work as a builder, needs to retrain
Emotional needs: has difficulty in coming to terms with disability

16-year-old

Social needs: has been in trouble with police for truancy and petty crime
Educational needs: needs to pass exams to go to art college
Physical needs: has acne
Emotional needs: depressed

New mother

Physical needs: problems with breastfeeding, needs to lose weight
Emotional needs: slight postnatal depression
Social needs: feels isolated in new town with new baby

Toddler

Physical needs: **immunisation,** regular checks on development
Social needs: needs contact with other children
Educational needs: needs stimulating environment in which to play and learn

In the next activity you will be thinking about how the health and social services might be able to help meet some of these needs.

Activity

Look back at the chart you created in the previous activity. This time, type or write in the column marked 'Service' which health or social service you think could meet the needs you have identified already. Remember to consider health care, education, social services and services provided by voluntary organisations and privately.

Could you think of a service for each need?
Here are some possibilities. You may have thought of others.

Elderly woman

Physical: home help from social services, free chiropody at health centre
Social: visits from Age Concern volunteer, tea dances run by church group
Educational: French classes at local college subsidised by local authority

Man in wheelchair

Physical: adaptations in the home, for example widening doorways and ramps for wheelchair with grant from local authority, physiotherapy at hospital, adapted car – bought privately with help from a charity
Educational: skills training programme run by local authority
Emotional: **counselling** from private counsellor

16-year-old

Educational: goes to school – **education welfare officer** ensures he attends
Social: probation officer gets him involved in local art project to stop him reoffending
Physical: GP prescribes cream for acne
Emotional: youth worker gives counselling twice a week

New mother

Physical: visits from health visitor to help with breastfeeding, postnatal exercise classes run by voluntary organisation
Emotional: counselling from GP
Social: baby clinic at health centre where she can meet other mothers
Educational: parentcraft classes at local college run by local authority

Toddler

Physical: immunisation and developmental checks at health centre
Social and educational: private playgroup

As you can see from these ideas, different types of people have different needs and there are different services to meet those needs. For example, most new mothers need support and advice from a health visitor. But no two people have exactly the same needs and it is up to health and social service workers to ensure that services are tailored as far as possible to people's individual needs. To do this they need to spend time talking with the people they work with so that they can find out what their needs are and how they can best be met. This is one of the things that makes working in health and social services interesting and enjoyable. In the next section we will be looking at the different kinds of jobs that health and social service workers do. The following activity gives you an opportunity to see what you already know about working in health and social services.

Activity

1 **Read the following quotations from people who work in health and social services about what they do. Try to match the quotations with this list of workers.**

- hospital midwife
- GP
- day care social worker
- education welfare officer
- health visitor
- home care assistant
- hospital consultant

- occupational therapist
- youth worker
- residential social worker
- speech therapist
- district nurse
- nursery nurse
- community psychiatric nurse

a 'I am in charge of patients' care while they are in hospital, working with a team of doctors and nurses.'

b 'I work in the maternity hospital, carrying out antenatal checks on pregnant women, delivering their babies and visiting them at home afterwards.'

c 'I visit people in their homes to work out what aids and adaptations they require and how best to provide them. Most of my clients are elderly but I also have some clients with disabilities.'

d 'I work in a residential home for children with severe learning difficulties.'

e 'I mainly work with children who play truant but I also give support and advice to parents who have problems which affect their children at school.'

f 'I help look after people in their own homes – doing the shopping, cooking, washing, cleaning or whatever needs to be done.'

g 'I treat people who have general health problems. For anything more serious I refer them to hospital.'

h 'I help people who have speech difficulties. I often work with children but I also help older people who have lost their speech after a stroke.'

i 'I provide nursing care in people's own homes, doing things like changing dressings, giving injections and taking out stitches.'

j 'I'm a trained nurse but I specialise in working with people at home – usually young families. I visit new mothers and try to help them with any problems they might have.'

k 'I visit people with mental health problems at home.'

l 'I work with young people, offering support, counselling and activities.'

m 'I work in a day centre for adults with disabilities, providing a range of activities. I'm the only paid worker – everyone else is a volunteer.'

n 'I help run a nursery for pre-school children. We do all kinds of things – painting, singing, dancing.'

The answers to this question are given at the end of this study unit (see page 190).

2   You may have met other health and social service workers yourself.
Write down any other jobs in health and social care that you can
think of.

Getting access to services

Although we are all entitled to the health and social services which
are provided by the welfare state, we cannot usually get what we need
unless someone who works in the health or social services arranges it
for us. For example, if you need to go to hospital you usually have to
be **referred** by a GP unless you pay privately. How we get access to
health, education and social services is explained in more detail next.

Gatekeepers

There are some health and social service professionals who act as
gatekeepers to other services. This means that they should know
what other services are available, who is entitled to them and how
to organise them if they are needed. There are three main types of
gatekeeper in health and social care:

- GPs
- social workers and/or care managers
- some **hospital specialists**.

Other professionals who can make sure people have access to
services include:

- community nurses such as district nurses, health visitors and
  community psychiatric nurses
- teachers
- occupational therapists.

Health   Most health services are provided free of charge although some of
us have to pay for prescriptions, dental care and chiropody and we
may have to wait for some services such as hospital treatment.
Some people pay for private health treatment.

Education

All children and young people between five and sixteen have the right to free education, although parents may be asked to help pay for some items. Many parents have to pay privately for nursery education before their children are five because there are not enough free places to go round. Some parents pay for their children to go to private schools.

Social services

Getting access to social services can be more difficult because they are aimed at the people most in need and are often overstretched. However, the *NHS and Community Care Act 1990* aims for everyone to be given the help they need in order to be able to live in the community – this concept is called **care in the community** or **community care**. Under this new legislation local authorities have a duty to **assess** what help people need and to arrange it for them if they can. Local authorities have different ways of organising community care but it is usually the responsibility of a social worker.

Some services are provided directly by the local authority and others are bought in from voluntary organisations or private companies.

There is often a charge for social services these days. The amount people are asked to pay towards the services they receive usually depends on how much money they have but every local authority has its own system of charging.

Activity

In this activity you will find out more about the social services listed opposite. If you can, contact your local social services office and for each of these services find out whether:

- they are provided free of charge
- if people have to pay for them, how the charge is calculated
- whether the services are provided directly by the social services office or bought in from other organisations.

Telephone the local social services office and ask to speak to an information officer. Explain that you are doing a GNVQ in health and social care and that you want to find out about how certain social services are provided in your area. He/she should be able to answer your questions or point you in the direction of someone who can.

The telephone number of the local social services office should be in the phone book under the name of your local authority.

Services

Residential home care

Day centre for people with disabilities

Pre-school nursery

Home care assistants (home helps)

Transport to a social services day centre

Aids and adaptations

Meals on wheels

Did you find out about all the services? It's not always easy to obtain this kind of information so don't worry if you didn't manage to complete the list.

In the rest of this section you will be working on a project to find out more about local services and who is entitled to them.

2.2, 2.4, 2.5 IT **C** **Project**

In this project you will be looking in more detail at the health and social care services in your area. This is a very long project and it may take some time to complete. Read the whole project through carefully before you begin doing any work.

It is in two parts:
- Part A looks at local services
- Part B looks at computer facilities.

In Part A you will be considering an imaginary example of someone who needs help and finding out what services he/she would be entitled to and how to get access to them. In Part B you will be looking at computer facilities and how well equipped an organisation in your area is.

Part A   1   **Read the four case studies which follow and choose one on which to base your project.**

Sarah is a fifteen-year-old who keeps running away from home

Jon is a two-year-old with behaviour problems

Paul is a 25-year-old with
Down's Syndrome

Flora is an 83-year-old
who has lived alone for
the past five years

175

Case study 1

Jon is a two-year-old boy with **behaviour problems**. His GP has said that he has **special needs.** His parents want him to go to a nursery for five mornings or afternoons a week, partly to allow Jon's mother to work part-time but also because they think it would be good for Jon to have a more structured day and to have an opportunity to be with other children.

Case study 2

Sarah is a 15-year-old girl who keeps running away from home. She is unruly and disruptive at school and most of the teachers find her very difficult to cope with. One teacher, however, gets on well with Sarah and is concerned that she is having problems at home. Her mother has never shown any interest in Sarah's progress (or problems) at school and Sarah once said something to the teacher which suggested that her stepfather had been sexually abusing her.

Case study 3

Paul is a 25-year-old man with **Down's Syndrome**. He has always lived with his parents but during the last two years they have both died. Since his mother died six months ago he has been staying with his sister but she is finding it difficult to manage everything as she works full time. Paul also wants to be more **independent.** He is able to do his own cleaning and washing but can't really manage shopping and cooking. He has inherited the house he lived in with his parents but he would prefer to move to something smaller and nearer to his sister, who lives 50 miles away.

Case study 4

Flora is an 83-year-old woman who has lived alone for the past five years since her husband died. She lives in a council flat on her retirement pension and a small private pension. She has a small amount of savings. She has recently recovered from a hip replacement operation and is finding it difficult to manage at home despite help from her family, friends and neighbours. She is nervous about leaving the flat on her own. She thinks she might like to move into sheltered housing.

2   **When you have chosen a case study, find out:**
   - what services might be available for the person in the case study including health services, social services and education
   - who provides them
   - whether the person would have to pay for, or towards, them.

   To do this you will need to:
   - talk to health and social care workers
   - refer to local sources of information.

Health and social care workers

You will also need to talk to some of the following health and social care workers, depending on which case study you have selected:
   - doctor
   - nurse
   - social worker
   - youth worker
   - pre-school nursery teacher
   - volunteer from a charity or voluntary organisation
   - someone who works for an organisation offering private health or social services.

Local sources of information

You should be able to get some of the information you need from one or more of the following local sources of information:
   - CAB
   - GP's surgery
   - health clinic
   - library.

You may be able to think of others too.

3 **Using a computer, write a care plan for the person you have selected based on the information you have found out about local health and social services. Look again at the care plan for George Robinson on page 156 to remind you of what your care plan should look like. Make sure it includes:**

You will have to make some assumptions about the person you have selected as you do not have all the information that a social worker would need to produce a real care plan.

- a brief description of the services which are available

- information about who would provide them

- whether the person would have to pay for, or towards, them.

Part B 1 **When you visit the *local sources of information* you have selected find out what computer facilities they have and decide which one is the best equipped. To do this, you will need to ask the people who work there what they think. The following list of questions might help you decide:**

- Are the computer facilities easy to use?

- Have they made the jobs of the people who work there easier?

- Do they save them time?

- Can they be used for data and graphics as well as text?

- Can computerised information be protected in any way (for example security routines such as passwords, back-up procedures)?

2 **If possible, arrange to spend a half day at the place which you have decided has the best IT facilities. This visit may need to be set up by your school or college. For this part of the project you will be looking at two aspects of working with computers:**

- health and safety

- how the computer system operates.

Use the following questionnaire (or draw up a similar one of your own) to find out as much as you can about these two aspects. It may be possible to use the computer system yourself and you will certainly need to talk to the people who work there.

PERSONAL DETAILS

Surname: Maiberg
Name: Jekaterina
Address: 43C Sandeman Street, Dundee
Post Code: DD3 7LE
Telephone number: 07828962873
Email: maiberg@mail.ru

EDUCATION

Secondary/Further/Higher Education, Qualifications gained or pending - subject and level	Date	Grade (if applicable)
Narva High School (Estonia)	1997 – 2000	HND
Sillamae Institute of Management and Economics	2000 – 2004	80 %
Dundee College (ESOL)	2006 – 2008	SAQ

PRESENT OR MOST RECENT EMPLOYMENT

Job Title: Personal carer assistant

Employer's name   Thamas Allan
and address: 21 Clement Park Road, Dundee, DD2 3NF

**Date of
Start:**   19.06.2007

**Date of
 Finish:**   02.08.2008

Reason for leaving: Clients passing away

KNOWLEDGE, SKILLS AND EXPERIENCE

Last 14 months I was working as a personal carer assistant for spinal injured person and my job included all aspects of care: bed bath giving, food preparation, use of hoist, dealing with medication and etc. I was working mostly on my own in the client's house. I consider myself as a reliable, responsible and passion person. I am good at working as a part of the team and on my own initiative. I am always excited and capable of learning new things and studying.

Health and safety

Questionnaire for project

1 Is the seating comfortable for people who use the computers?

2 Is the lighting adequate and arranged so that there is no glare on the computer screens?

3 Are the screens arranged so that they are not facing windows?

4 Are they arranged at a height which is comfortable for the people using them so they don't have to hunch over or bend forward to see?

5 Are there cables on the floor which people might trip over?

6 Is there any system to protect the computer system from computer 'viruses'?

7 What measures have been taken to ensure that the computer equipment is not damaged?

How the computer system operates

1 How is information stored on the computer? Find out what software is used and how to use it.

2 How is information on the computer edited?

3 How is information from different sources organised on the computer (for example, from other offices or organisations)?

4 What software is available for presenting different kinds of information (for example, spreadsheets, graphics packages)?

5 What is the procedure if someone makes an error or there is a fault on the computer?

6 How are other people notified of the fault or error?

7 What safety precautions are taken to protect people and information on the machines during repairs?

8 Are there procedures for saving and backing up information?

If you are not sure about how to plan your project, look again at the induction booklet for Intermediate level.

Your project will form part of the evidence in your portfolio.

People's rights in health and social care

So far in this study unit we have looked at:

- what health and social care services are available
- how people get access to them.

In the last section of this unit we will be looking at what **rights** people have when they use health and care services.

Activity

1 Write down your own definition starting with the words 'A right is ...'.

2 In a group or on your own, think about what we mean by the word 'right'. What is a right? Look it up in a dictionary if you want to and discuss the definition given there.

3 Think of as many different types of rights as you can and write a list of them, for example freedom of religion, freedom of speech.

The *Longman Dictionary of the English Language* gives this definition of 'right':

'in accordance with what is **morally** good, just or proper'.

This definition is probably easier to understand:

'A right is something that we are entitled to by law or morally.'

Did you think of many different types of rights? We came up with the following list:

- the right to freedom of speech
- the right to freedom from discrimination
- the right to freedom of choice
- the right to dignity
- the right to independence
- the right to **confidentiality**
- the right to information
- the right to complain
- the right to health
- the right to safety
- the right to be treated as an individual.

It is the responsibility of health and social care workers to ensure that these rights are maintained when we use health and social care services. In the next activity you will be looking at ways in which our rights can be threatened when we use health and social care services.

1 Read the three scenarios which follow.

2 For each one identify which type of right it is concerned with.

3 Decide how the person's right is being threatened by the situation.

Scenario 1

Mrs Virk is an 80-year-old Asian woman who needs to go into a residential home. Her social worker has recommended one particular home because she says a number of Asian people live there and that the other homes in the area are not so 'geared up' for Asian people. She offers to take Mrs Virk to see the home.

Scenario 2

Anne is a 45-year-old woman who has been diagnosed as having breast cancer. The hospital consultant says that she should have a **mastectomy** – an operation to have her breast removed. She feels very distressed by this idea and finds the consultant difficult to talk to. She is particularly uncomfortable about asking him how she will look and feel after a mastectomy. She also feels that no-one has properly explained to her what the alternatives are. In the end she agrees to have a mastectomy.

Scenario 3

Gwenda is a 35-year-old receptionist in a health centre. One morning she accidentally overhears part of a conversation between one of the doctors and a female patient who tells the doctor that her husband is beating her regularly. Gwenda recognises the woman as a neighbour and is quite shocked as the couple have always seemed happy and settled. She is careful not to mention this to anyone at the health centre although when she gets home she tells her own husband.

These scenarios are examples of threats on three different types of rights:

Scenario 1 threatens Mrs Virk's *right to freedom from discrimination.* Although the social worker may have been trying to be helpful, she is assuming that because Mrs Virk is Asian she will automatically want to be with other Asian people. By only offering to take Mrs Virk to that particular home she is also threatening both her right to be an individual and her freedom of choice.

Scenario 2 threatens Anne's *right to information.* The consultant should have ensured that Anne was given all the information she needed in order to decide whether or not to have the mastectomy. He is also threatening her right to freedom of choice because he has not explained the alternatives to her.

Scenario 3 threatens the patient's *right to confidentiality.* Although Gwenda was careful not to mention the conversation she had overheard to anyone else at the health centre, she should not have told her husband, even if he had promised not to tell anyone else. The patient had the right to assume that in the doctor's surgery anything she said was confidential.

Activity

1 Re-read Scenario 1 in which Mrs Virk is pressurised by her social worker to select a particular residential care home.

2 In a group or on your own, think about ways in which the social worker could have ensured that Mrs Virk's rights were maintained.

The social worker could have provided Mrs Virk with a list of four or five homes and offered to take her to see all of them before she made her choice. The social worker could also have found out from Mrs Virk beforehand whether she had a preference to be with other Asian people or whether this was not one of her most important requirements when looking for a home.

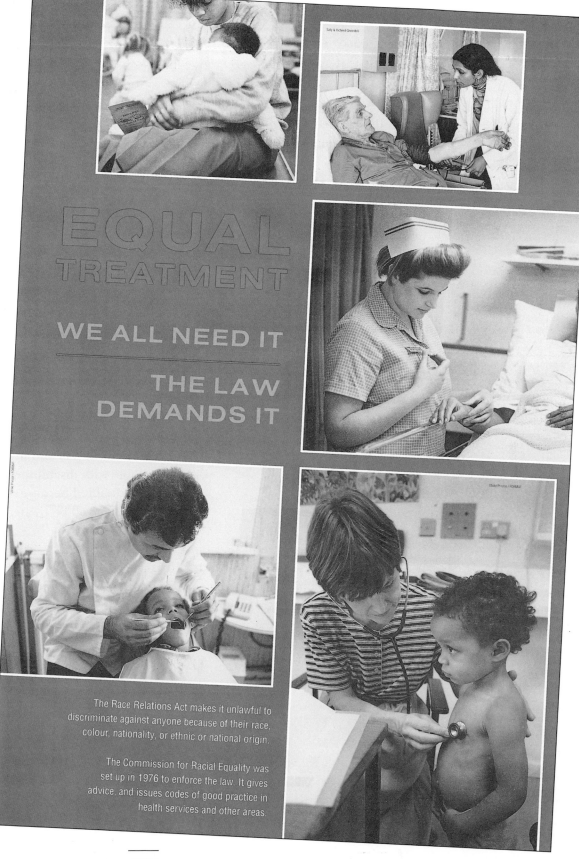

EQUAL
TREATMENT

WE ALL NEED IT

THE LAW
DEMANDS IT

The Race Relations Act makes it unlawful to discriminate against anyone because of their race, colour, nationality, or ethnic or national origin.

The Commission for Racial Equality was set up in 1976 to enforce the law. It gives advice, and issues codes of good practice in health services and other areas.

In the UK, there are laws to protect people from some kinds of discrimination:

Sex discrimination

The Sex Discrimination Acts 1975 and *1986* make it illegal to discriminate against someone on account of whether he/she is a man or woman and whether he/she is married or not.

Race discrimination

The Race Relations Act 1976 makes it illegal to discriminate against someone on account of his/her colour, race, nationality or beliefs and/or customs.

Discrimination against people with disabilities

The Disabled Persons (Employment) Act 1944 requires employers with 20 or more workers to employ 3 per cent of registered disabled people in their workforces. (In fact, this law is usually ignored by employers and in any case, many people with disabilities do not register as disabled because they think they will be treated as 'abnormal'.)

Discrimination against children

The Children Act 1989 gives children the right to be listened to and the right to make a complaint, among other rights.

ECONOMIC, SOCIAL, CULTURAL AND PROTECTIVE RIGHTS

These cover the child's rights to proper standards of physical care, education, health and protection from harm.

Rights to life
Children have a right to life and to the best possible chance to develop fully (*Article 6*).

Standards of living
Every child has the right to an adequate standard of living. This is, in the main, for parents to provide, but in cases of need the Government should help parents reach this standard (*Article 27*). Every child has the right to benefit from social security taking account of the resources and circumstances of the child and those responsible for the child (*Article 26*).

Day to day care
The Convention says children should be cared for properly from day to day. This is mainly for the child's parents to do but the Government is expected to give suitable help to parents (*Article 18*).

If children cannot live with their family, they must be properly looked after by another family or in a children's home. The child's race, religion, culture and language must all be considered when a new home is being chosen for the child (*Article 20*).

2.3 IT **C** **Activity**

Using a computer, design a poster or leaflet giving people information about their rights to freedom from discrimination. It could be on sex discrimination, race discrimination, discrimination against people with disabilities or discrimination against children (or all four).

Activity

1   Re-read Scenario 2 in which Anne is told she has breast cancer.

2   In a group or on your own, think about ways in which the consultant and other hospital staff could have ensured that Anne was given all the information she needed to make an informed choice.

In some hospitals there is a nurse or counsellor who specialises in giving advice and support to women who have been diagnosed as having breast cancer. The consultant could have given Anne information about one of the cancer charities, most of which have helplines and information leaflets. Also, he could have put her in touch with a local mastectomy support group or other women who had had a mastectomy and were prepared to talk to Anne about their experiences.

Activity

1   Re-read Scenario 3 in which a doctor's receptionist breached a patient's right to confidentiality.

2   In a group or on your own think about why it is important not to give anyone confidential information about patients or clients when you work in health or social care. List as many reasons as you can.

People who care for others as part of their job – doctors, nurses, social workers and so on – often have to handle very confidential information about the people they work with. They have to make sure that this information is only ever used to benefit the people in their care and that information is not disclosed without good reason.

There are three main reasons why the right to confidentiality is important:

- People who need health or social care may have to disclose very private information that they wouldn't normally give to anyone else.
- It is important to keep the information confidential because some people might not use it for the benefit of the patient or client if they had access to it.
- People need to be able to trust health and social care workers.

In the rest of this section you will be working on a project in which you will find out how someone working in a local health or social care service makes sure that his/her patients' or clients' rights are protected.

Project

In this project you will find out about rights. It will involve:

- interviewing a health or social care worker about how they protect the rights of their patients or clients
- writing some guidelines for that worker's patients or clients on their rights when using the service.

To complete this project you will probably need to follow these steps:

1 **Find someone who is willing to talk to you about his/her work and the rights of his/her patients or clients. For example, you might be able to interview a doctor, nurse, health visitor, social worker, nursery worker, day centre worker or residential care worker. The interview may need to be set up by your school or college.**

2 **Write a letter on a computer explaining why you want to interview him/her and what you hope to get out of the interview. Explain that you are doing a GNVQ on health and social care and that your project is about people's rights when using health and social care services.**

3 **Prepare a list of questions for the interview. You will need to find out:**

- What kind of person the worker usually works with – for example, is most of the work to do with elderly people, children, people with disabilities, etc.?
- What services the worker provides – for example, nursing care, advice and support, training, etc.

- Whether the organisation they work for has a policy on discrimination.
- How they personally try to make sure that:
  - none of the patients or clients are discriminated against
  - the patients or clients get the information they need
  - confidential information about their patients or clients is kept confidential.
- What happens if a client or patient wants to complain?

4 **After the interview, type and print out a letter on a computer to the worker to thank them for seeing you.**

5 **Using a computer, write and print out some guidelines for the worker's patients or clients based on what the worker has told you about their rights when using the service. Use the following headings to structure the guidelines:**
- whom the guidelines are for (the client or patient group)
- the service provided by the worker
- the policy on discrimination
- how clients/patients' rights are maintained:
  - the right to freedom from discrimination
  - the right to information
  - the right to confidentiality
- how to make a complaint.

If you are not sure about how to plan your project, have another look at the induction booklet which came with this study unit.

Your project will form part of the evidence in your portfolio.

Summary

This study unit has introduced you to the way in which health and social services are organised and to some of the different jobs that are involved, such as health visitors, GPs, community nurses and social workers. The health and social services aim to work together but you have seen that the structure is complex and the relationships between them can be complicated.

You have also looked at how the services meet the needs of different groups in the community and how people get access to them. Your knowledge of how the services are organised and how to find your way around them will help you to ensure that you (and your clients) can get the best from the services available.

Finally, you have considered the different rights people should have when using the services and how health and social care workers can help to make sure that these rights are maintained. Your awareness of these rights will help you to be sensitive to the needs of others and to promote awareness in others.

Review activity

You have now completed your work on this study unit. You should now spend some time reviewing what you have achieved.

1 Grading themes

For Intermediate GNVQs you can achieve a higher grading depending on how much initiative and independent action you take in the areas of:

- planning
- information-gathering.

Action planning

Look over all the projects you worked on for this unit:

- Did you complete detailed action plans for each project?
- How much support did you need from your teacher/tutor to complete the plans?
- Did you regularly review and update your plans?

- How successful were you in achieving your plans and targets?
- Were there any areas where you didn't achieve your plans? Why was this?
- What would you have done differently?

Information-gathering

Look over all the projects you worked on for this unit:

- Did you successfully identify the sorts of information you needed to complete projects and activities?
- Did you successfully gather the information you needed? How did you do this?
- How would you assess the quality of information you gathered? Was it:
  - useful and relevant?
  - appropriate for your needs?
  - accurate and complete?
- Were there any areas where you were not able to gather the information you needed? Why was this?
- What would you have done differently?

2 Performance criteria and range

Look at the standards for this GNVQ unit. Work through the PCs for the unit and check that you have done work that will help you meet each one. Do this by noting down the PC number against the relevant work.

Finally check through the information given under the range.

- Do you understand everything that is listed in the range?
- Are you confident that the work you have done on projects covers the range properly?

3 Core skills

This unit has covered the following core skills:

- Communication Elements 2.3 and 2.4
- Application of Number Elements 2.2 and 2.3
- Information Technology Elements 2.2, 2.3, 2.4 and 2.5

Answers to activities

page 149   Your answer should have looked like this:

Health service	Social service
baby clinic	residential home for old people
chiropody	nursery
GP	meals on wheels
hospital physiotherapy	day centre for people with
optician	disabilities
	social services transport

page 169, question 1

a hospital consultant

b hospital midwife

c occupational therapist

d residential social worker

e education welfare officer

f home care assistant

g GP

h speech therapist

i district nurse

j health visitor

k community psychiatric nurse

l youth worker

m day care social worker

n nursery nurse

Although this isn't a complete list, it should give you an idea of some of the types of jobs in health and social services that people do.

Glossary

assess in social care services, someone who appears to need help is 'assessed' in order to decide what help, if any, they need

behaviour problems someone who is behaving in an anti-social or disruptive way is said to have behaviour problems

care in the community a new idea introduced into the UK in recent years, care in the community aims to enable people to live in the community rather than in residential care

care manager a health or social care worker appointed to co-ordinate the services to be provided to someone

care plan a document summarising the health and social care services to be provided to someone

cerebral palsy a condition in which muscles and limbs do not function properly as a result of brain damage before or during birth

charity a non-profit-making organisation set up to give help to people who need it

chiropody care of the feet

community care *see* **care in the community**

community psychiatric nurse (CPN) a nurse with special psychiatric training who visits people with mental health problems at home to give them advice and sometimes medication

confidential something spoken, written or given in confidence; secret or private

consultant *see* **hospital consultant**

coronary bypass operation operation to replace an artery to the heart with a vein from the leg

counselling working with people to help them to find solutions to their problems; giving advice or guidance

discrimination unfair treatment of a person or group

district nurse a nurse who provides nursing care at home

Down's syndrome a genetic abnormality which causes learning difficulties

education welfare officer a social worker who specialises in working with children who are having difficulties at school and their parents and teachers; ensures that children attend school

gatekeeper in health and social care services, someone who helps people get the services they need

gross expenditure level of spending before expenses

health visitor a nurse who works with people in their own homes, especially young families

home care assistant provides practical help at home such as cooking and cleaning; may also help with personal care such as bathing

hospital consultant a specialist doctor who works in a hospital; patients are under the care of a consultant while they are in hospital

hospital specialist examples of hospital specialists are paediatricians, who specialise in the treatment of children, and geriatricians, who specialise in the treatment of older people. *See also* **hospital consultant**

immunisation protection against a disease, usually by injection

independent free from control; not dependent on anything or anyone else

local authority council which is responsible for local government

mastectomy an operation to remove a breast

midwife a nurse who works with pregnant women and delivers their babies

morality particular principles of right and wrong; an ethical code

national insurance state insurance paid by employers and employees to provide benefits for unemployed people, retired people and people who are sick or disabled

occupational therapy help for people who have been disabled to enable them to manage everyday tasks; advice and provision of aids and adaptations

ophthalmology the branch of medicine concerned with the eye and diseases of the eye

pharmaceutical a drug or medicine

physiotherapy treatment for and advice about relieving pain and restoring mobility

prescribe to recommend or order the use of a drug or medicine

primary healthcare the first level of healthcare – usually our first point of contact; mainly provided by GPs, dentists, community nurses such as district nurses and health visitors

probation officer someone who supervises and helps offenders who are on probation

providers under the purchaser/provider system the providers (hospitals, GPs) supply health care to the purchasers

purchaser the name for organisations such as district health authorities and family health service authorities which buy health services from, for example, trust hospitals and GPs

refer in healthcare, to direct someone for treatment elsewhere; for example a GP refers a patient to a hospital

right something to which we are entitled by law or morally

secondary healthcare the second level of healthcare for patients who need more care or treatment than can be provided by **primary healthcare**; usually provided by hospitals

social education centre a day centre where people with learning difficulties can learn new skills and get help and advice

special needs someone who needs particular services; for example, someone with learning difficulties

speech therapist someone who is trained to help people overcome speech difficulties

trust an independent unit within the NHS

voluntary organisation *see* **charity**

welfare state a system in which the state is responsible for making sure that people are cared for in terms of their health and welfare

Index

Acknowledgements

Photographic Acknowledgements

BTEC; page 99
Bubbles; page 165 *bottom*
Chubb Ltd; page 138
Department of Health; page 184
Sally and Richard Greenhill; page 28, page 34 *bottom*, page 36, page 39, page 42, page 50, page 55 *centre and top left*, page 62, page 79, page 88, page 91, page 147, page 165 *top centre, middle left and right*
Hulton Deutsch; page 146
Photofusion; page 34 *top*, page 74
Photofusion/Gina Glover; page 27, page 55 *top right*
Photofusion/Crispin Hughes; page 69
Sam Tanner; page 150